American Birding Association
Field Guide to Birds
of Pennsylvania

American Birding Association

Field Guide

to Birds of

Pennsylvania

George L. Armistead

PHOTOGRAPHS BY
Brian E. Small
AND OTHERS

Scott & Nix, Inc.
NEW YORK

PUBLISHED BY SCOTT & NIX, INC.
150 W 28TH ST, STE 1900
NEW YORK, NY 10001
SCOTTANDNIX.COM

FIRST EDITION 2015

ISBN 978-1-935622-52-9

AMERICAN BIRDING ASSOCIATION, INC.
800-850-2473
ABA.ORG

SCOTT & NIX, INC. BOOKS
ARE DISTRIBUTED TO THE TRADE BY:

INDEPENDENT PUBLISHERS GROUP (IPG)
814 NORTH FRANKLIN STREET
CHICAGO, IL 60610
800-888-4741
IPGBOOK.COM

PRINTED IN CHINA

Contents

The American Birding Association inspires all people to enjoy and protect wild birds.

The ABA represents the North American birding community and supports birders through publications, conferences, workshops, events, partnerships, and networks.

The ABA's education programs promote birding skills, ornithological knowledge, and the development of and implementation of a conservation ethic.

The ABA encourages birders to apply their skills to help conserve birds and their habitats, and we represent the interests of birders in planning and legislative arenas.

We welcome all birders as members.

THE AMERICAN BIRDING ASSOCIATION
CODE OF ETHICS

Everyone who enjoys birds and birding must always respect wildlife, its environment, and the rights of others. In any conflict of interest between birds and birders, the welfare of the birds and their environment comes first.

CODE OF BIRDING ETHICS

1. Promote the welfare of birds and their environment.

    1(a) Support the protection of important bird habitat.

    1(b) To avoid stressing birds or exposing them to danger, exercise restraint and caution during observation, photography, sound recording, or filming.

Limit the use of recordings and other methods of attracting birds, and never use such methods in heavily birded areas, or for attracting any species that is Threatened, Endangered, or of Special Concern, or is rare in your local area; Keep well back from nests and nesting colonies, roosts, display areas, and important feeding sites. In such sensitive areas, if there is a need for extended observation, photography, filming, or recording, try to use a blind or hide, and take advantage of natural cover.

Use artificial light sparingly for filming or photography, especially for close-ups.

1(c) Before advertising the presence of a rare bird, evaluate the potential for disturbance to the bird, its surroundings, and other people in the area, and proceed only if access can be controlled, disturbance minimized, and permission has been obtained from private land-owners. The sites of rare nesting birds should be divulged only to the proper conservation authorities.

1(d) Stay on roads, trails, and paths where they exist; otherwise keep habitat disturbance to a minimum.

2. Respect the law, and the rights of others.

2(a) Do not enter private property without the owner's explicit permission.

2(b) Follow all laws, rules, and regulations governing use of roads and public areas, both at home and abroad.

2(c) Practice common courtesy in contacts with other people. Your exemplary behavior will generate goodwill with birders and non-birders alike.

3. Ensure that feeders, nest structures, and other artificial bird environments are safe.

3(a) Keep dispensers, water, and food clean, and free of decay or disease. It is important to feed birds continually during harsh weather.

3(b) Maintain and clean nest structures regularly.

3(c) If you are attracting birds to an area, ensure the birds are not exposed to predation from cats and other domestic animals, or dangers posed by artificial hazards.

4. Group birding, whether organized or impromptu, requires special care.

Each individual in the group, in addition to the obligations spelled out in Items 1 and 2, has responsibilities as a Group Member.

4(a) Respect the interests, rights, and skills of fellow birders, as well as people participating in other legitimate outdoor activities. Freely share your knowledge and experience, except where code 1(c) applies. Be especially helpful to beginning birders.

4(b) If you witness unethical birding behavior, assess the situation, and intervene if you think it prudent. When interceding, inform the person(s) of the inappropriate action, and attempt, within reason, to have it stopped. If the behavior continues, document it, and notify appropriate individuals or organizations.

Group Leader Responsibilities [amateur and professional trips and tours].

4(c) Be an exemplary ethical role model for the group. Teach through word and example.

4(d) Keep groups to a size that limits impact on the environment, and does not interfere with others using the same area.

4(e) Ensure everyone in the group knows of and practices this code.

4(f) Learn and inform the group of any special circumstances applicable to the areas being visited (e.g. no tape recorders allowed).

4(g) Acknowledge that professional tour companies bear a special responsibility to place the welfare of birds and the benefits of public knowledge ahead of the company's commercial interests. Ideally, leaders should keep track of tour sightings, document unusual occurrences, and submit records to appropriate organizations.

Everyone who enjoys birds and birding must always respect wildlife, its environment, and the rights of others. The ABA Code of Ethics should be read, followed, and shared by all birders.

Please follow this code and distribute and teach it to others.

The American Birding Association's Code of Birding Ethics may be freely reproduced for distribution/dissemination. An electronic version may be found at aba.org/about/ethics.

Foreword

Whether you're backpacking through the Allegheny National Forest, paddling a tributary of the Susquehanna, waiting for a bus in downtown Pittsburgh, or gazing out the window onto a suburban backyard, there are birds to look at, to enjoy, and to learn about in Pennsylvania.

That's where this book comes in. Like all the guides in the ABA State series, it can help you do whatever you want with birding. Perhaps you enjoy birds a few days a year in your yard or local park and just want to know a little more and to know their names. Or maybe you want to dive deeper and really get familiar with the many amazing birds of Pennsylvania. However you approach it, birding is a peerless way to leave your cares behind and become more alive to what is going on all around you, every day.

George Armistead, who wrote this book, has been birding since he was a little boy in downtown Philadelphia, a place he still calls home. He was born into a well-known birding family and devoted much of his life to worldwide travel as a professional bird tour leader. He's a perfect guide for Keystone State birding at any level of interest.

As you make your way into birding, I invite you to visit the American Birding Association web-site (aba.org), where you'll find a wealth of free resources and ways to connect with the birding community that will also help you get the most from your birding in Pennsylvania and beyond. Please consider becoming an ABA member yourself—one of the best parts of birding is joining a community of fun, passionate people.

Now get on out there! Enjoy this book. Enjoy Pennsylvania. And most of all, enjoy birding!

Good birding,

Jeffrey A. Gordon

Jeffrey A. Gordon, *President*
American Birding Association

Birds and Birders in Pennsylvania

From the ridges of the Appalachian Mountains to the tree-lined rivers in the mountain valleys, from the sandy shores of Lake Erie to the low-lying southeastern Piedmont, and across our endless expanses of lush forest, "Penn's Woods" is a delightful region for birding.

Over half the state is cloaked in forest, not so different from its habitats when William Penn was granted the charter in 1681, but of course so much else has changed. During the 1800s, vast sections of woods were harvested, yet still a few remnants of gorgeous old-growth forest remain. A visit to Cook Forest State Park will reveal 150-foot-tall trees, and at the Tionesta Natural Area visitors can commune with 500-year-old hemlocks. Pennsylvania remains one of the country's top lumber producers, but it hosts a wide variety of other habitats.

The Appalachian Mountains extend from the Allegheny Mountains in the southwest toward the northeast to the Poconos. Northwest of this mountain chain is an elevated plateau. Southeast is the lower, arable Piedmont, and then a small sliver of coastal plain. The wilds of the forested plateau, the rolling ridges and valleys of the mountains, the lakes and rivers, and even the urban and suburban areas of Philadelphia and Pittsburgh provide many opportunities to encounter birds throughout the year.

Wood Ducks are among the commonwealth's most abundant breeding waterfowl. From March to October this beautiful duck is found near ponds, lakes, and rivers with adjacent woodlands.

The Keystone State has one of America's richest histories in American bird studies. The "father of American ornithology," Alexander Wilson, made his home in Philadelphia, and the historic city was dubbed by Roger Tory Peterson as "the cradle of American ornithology." Pennsylvania inspired Wilson's work, and it has been home to an unparalleled cadre of ornithological luminaries. John James Audubon, John Cassin, William Bartram, Witmer Stone, George Miksch Sutton, and James Bond called it home, as have more modern experts such as W. E. Clyde Todd, Earl L. Poole, Kenneth Parkes, Frank Gill, Robert S. Ridgely, and Scott Weidensaul. This rich tradition flourishes as the commonwealth continues to host a vibrant and active community of bird enthusiasts.

If you've picked up this book, you have at least a passing interest in the state's birds, and we hope this guide will further that interest. This is a reference to help you identify the birds common to this great state, and to make your birding even more rewarding.

Birds in this Guide

As of 2015, the official list of birds recorded in Pennsylvania is some 426 species. Many of these species nest here, some remain year-round, others occur only in winter, and other types migrate here during the spring and fall. Rarely some species occur only as wayward strays. This guide covers 252 annual species in Pennsylvania. They are a selection of our regularly encountered birds, a potpourri of year-round residents, migrant species, and nearly all the birds that routinely nest in the state.

Each species account in this guide gives the official English common and scientific name of the bird as determined by the Check-list of the American Ornithologists' Union (AOU). The accounts are arranged in the guide roughly in the order set forth by the AOU, which reflects the current scientific understanding of birds' evolution and relationships to one another.

The length and the wingspan in inches for each bird species is included in the accounts. The length measures from the tip of the bill to the end of the tail and the wingspan measures from the tip of the outermost flight feather from one side of the wing across the back to the other wingtip. There can be considerable variation in the size of individual birds of the same species based on gender, age, or even location. The measurements given in this guide are of average adult birds and are sourced from Birds of North America Online (bna.birds.cornell.edu) and All About Birds (allaboutbirds.org), both websites from the Cornell Lab of Ornithology in Ithaca, New York. These sites are excellent resources for more detailed information about bird life across North America.

Each species account contains text with information on the bird's "status," meaning how common the species is overall. There is also text about the bird's spatial (where) and temporal (when) distribution, referring to the geographic areas where the species lives and the time of year when it may be found.

Typically, notes in each account describe the bird's behavior, which is often related to its preferred habitat. In addition to the images, the text and captions direct readers to physical characteristics useful in identification, and sometimes how these compare with similar species.

Many accounts offer suggestions for birding hotspots to search for a particular type of bird. These are starter suggestions; usually there are many suitable places to see the species.

Identifying Birds

When you see a bird and wonder what it is, you may instinc-tively focus on color. Our best known birds such as the Blue Jay and the Northern Cardinal sport flashy colors, making them easy to spot and identify. Yet many birds are studies in brown and gray, and only careful scrutiny reveals their subtly beau-tiful color patterns. Generally, when trying to identify a bird, color is helpful, but there are many other useful points of reference, such as shape, size, habitats, time of year, time of day, vocalizations, and behavior. Paying attention to all of these factors will increase your enjoyment of identifying birds and make you a better birder.

Birds are creatures of habit with specific needs. Just as you have your day-to-day routine, so do birds. Some are found only in wooded areas, and others only in wetlands. Others are seldom away from open country, and some we see only when they fly past overhead. When you encounter a bird, study what you can of its plumage colors and patterns, its shape, size, and movements. Then, take a second look to zoom out and note its surroundings. Often a bird's habitat can tell you as much as the color of its feathering. Great Blue Herons stalk the water's edge. Horned Larks are out in fields with open ground. Chimney Swifts are seen rocketing around in the sky overhead, while Warbling Vireos occupy trees along rivers. These birds and many others are predictable this way, such that habitat and behavior are shortcuts in bird identification.

The Louisiana Waterthrush's preferred habitat is salong wooded creeks and streams from April to October. During the spring and early summer, it is especially vocal at dawn, but may be heard throughout the day. The combination of time of year, habitat, and this bird's distinctive song are prime identifiers.

Another useful identification tool is sound. Many people balk
at learning bird sounds, but this is not so difficult as it may
seem. Just as you can recognize the sound of your best friend's
voice, you can recognize the Carolina Wren, the American
Robin, or the Song Sparrow. Learn one or two common bird
sounds, and soon recognizing others gradually becomes easier.
When you hear a sound, guess what it is, and then try to see the
bird to test yourself. For many birds, the best way to find them
is by listening for their sounds. And listening doesn't mean that
you must memorize their vocalizations, but only that you have
a "search image" from which to work.

Another key to identifying birds is timing. Certain birds
remain in Pennsylvania all of their life, never venturing more
than a few miles from where they hatched. But some individuals undertake almost unimaginable migrations each year,
traveling thousands of miles from nesting areas in Canada or
Alaska to wintering areas in South America. Along the way,
they navigate dangerous city skylines, traverse immense bodies
of water, and avoid predators and inclement weather as much
as possible. Many travel only at night. These migrants are in
Pennsylvania only during this passage, headed north in spring
and south in fall.

Just as the time of year is important, so is the time of day. Owls
and nightjars are famously nocturnal, but many other birds are
active at night, while others are crepuscular (active at dawn
and dusk). As night draws to a close, certain places in spring
and summer unleash spectacular dawn choruses with a
cacophony of bird song. Many quit singing in mid-morning, but
certain species sing throughout the day. Midday is when the sun
can create rising columns of air that provide good conditions
for soaring birds to lift off and soar. Take a minute to consider
timing of the day and the season as you observe birds, and the
practice will reward you.

The female (left) and male (right) Red-winged Blackbird, one of the most abundant of all birds in North America, is an example of extreme sexual dimorphism—the female and the male have a dramatically different appearance throughout the year.

In some species, females and males differ dramatically in appearance. When males and females differ, they are sexually dimorphic. Sexual dimorphism occurs in many groups of birds, such as ducks and certain songbirds. We see it less among herons or shorebirds. In birds such as wrens, the females, males, and juveniles (birds born and fledged that year) all appear similar. For gulls, most shorebirds, and hawks, youngsters appear very different from their parents. In certain migrant species, only immature and nonbreeding birds are seen in Pennsylvania. Birders who appreciate how age and sex play a role in a bird's appearance and behavior will find bird identification easier.

Parts of a Bird

Though highly technical terms have been avoided as much as possible in the main text and captions of this guide, some special terms are used from time to time. The following illustrations with captions point out the prominent aspects of four major groups of birds: ducks, gulls, raptors, and songbirds.

PARTS OF A DUCK

When at rest, birds like this Redhead sometimes conceal their wing tips.

crown

forehead

nape

back

tail

bill

rump

flank

chest

PARTS OF A GULL

On this Laughing Gull, we can see the long black wing tips extending above and beyond the white, down-tilted tail.

eye crescent

bill

hood

mantle

upperwing coverts

gape

wing tips

chest

tail

undertail

belly

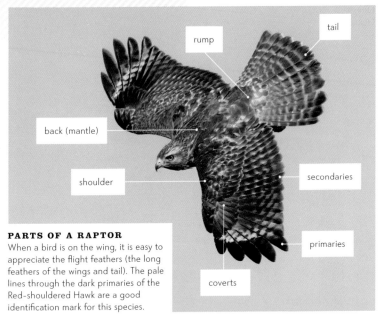

rump

tail

back (mantle)

shoulder

secondaries

primaries

coverts

PARTS OF A RAPTOR
When a bird is on the wing, it is easy to appreciate the flight feathers (the long feathers of the wings and tail). The pale lines through the dark primaries of the Red-shouldered Hawk are a good identification mark for this species.

tail

wing tip

undertail

wing bar

iris

pupil

lores

bill

PARTS OF A SONGBIRD
Many birds have "wing bars" like this White-eyed Vireo. The pale cream-colored tips of the wing coverts contrast with the darker bases, to create the "bars."

Often birds can be identified by a good study of the head and bill. Look at the features of this White-throated Sparrow, including its boldly patterned head.

crown stripe

eye line

eyebrow

cheek

lore

nape

back

moustachial stripe

chest

coverts

rump

flank

tail

wing tip

Birding in Pennsylvania

According to eBird (www.ebird.org), the popular online checklist and database program for recording bird sightings, Pennsylvania ranks sixth in the U.S. in terms of eBird checklists submitted by state. Only California, New York, Texas, Florida, and Massachusetts have more sightings submitted.

Within our state, Bucks and Lancaster counties share top honors for the highest species diversity (each with about 340 species per county), and these are followed fairly closely by Erie, Delaware, Berks, Centre, and Philadelphia. Erie is home to the birding hotspot with the highest list of species, with Presque Isle State Park at 314 and counting. It is followed by the John Heinz National Wildlife Refuge in Philadelphia, Peace Valley Park (Bucks), Yellow Creek State Park (Indiana), Bald Eagle State Park (Centre), Green Lane Reservoir (Montgomery), the legendary Conejohela Flats (Lancaster), and Middle Creek Wildlife Management Area (Lancaster).

During the warmer months, the wet woodlands and brushy thickets of the northwest and the Plateau are excellent areas to see the Northern Parula, one of the most widespread breeding warblers in the commonwealth.

These locations are rich in species diversity with long lists of fascinating birds, but there are many excellent bird-rich spots scattered across the state. Allegheny County, including Pittsburgh and its surroundings, has perhaps the most active birding community with the most checklists submitted to eBird. It is followed by Centre, Chester, Bucks, Montgomery, Lancaster, and Philadelphia counties. But many great places are seldom visited by bird enthusiasts. Birdwatchers interested in more pioneering efforts might focus on Cameron, Sullivan, or Elk counties, where few birders have recorded sightings.

The exquisite and abundant Northern Pintail may be found sometimes in large numbers on the open water of the northwest, including hotspots such as Presque Isle State Park.

NORTHWEST AND THE LAKE ERIE LAKESHORE Often referred to in the text as the northwest, for the purposes of this book, this area includes Erie, Crawford and Mercer counties.

Hotspots: Presque Isle State Park, Lake Pymatuning area

PLATEAU This is the largest region, comprising most of the western half of the state (except the northwest) and most of the northern half, too. It includes the Allegheny Plateau. The area in the text referred to as the southwest is the area from Johnstown west, and south of I-80, and includes Pittsburgh.

Hotspots: Yellow Creek State Park, Lake Somerset, Moraine State Park, Cook Forest State Park

Hawk Mountain Sanctuary is a premiere location to observe migrating raptors, such as this American Kestrel, during the fall and spring.

MOUNTAINS AND VALLEYS At times referred to only as the "mountains" in the text this includes the Appalachian ranges of the Allegheny mountains and the Poconos which run in a band from the south central part of the state, bend north and east across the east half of the state, reaching the Delaware River. The Allegheny Front sits on the western edge of the mountains and valleys and to its west is the Allegheny Plateau.

Hotspots: Shawnee State Park, Bald Eagle State Park, Waggoner's Gap, Hawk Mountain Sanctuary, Bake Oven Knob, Pocono Lake Preserve, Delaware Water Gap

PIEDMONT A word that translates into "at the foot of the mountains" this region is nestled into the southeastern part of the state between the mountains and the coastal plain.

Hotspots: Peace Valley Park, Lake Nockamixon, Green Lane Reservoir, Struble Lake, Lake Ontelaunee, Susquehanna River sites, Middle Creek Wildlife Management Area

True to its name, the Marsh Wren nests in wetland habitats of the Coastal Plain, as well as marshes of the northeast.

COASTAL PLAIN The smallest region, confined to the extreme southeastern part of the state, includes Philadelphia, and the flat low elevation areas surrounding it, below the Piedmont. This area combined with the Piedmont is referred to as the "southeast."

Hotspots: John Heinz (Tinicum) National Wildlife Refuge, Wissahickon Valley Park (Fairmount Park), Pennypack on the Delaware, Silver Lake Nature Center

A Year of Birding

As the calendar year unfolds, the composition of species in the state changes with the seasons. Below is a brief summary of general birdlife trends over the year, with birding hotspots recommended for each month. The hotspots mentioned represent just a few of the many places in the state that provide good bird-watching during this time.

JANUARY Though species diversity is low in January, the birding can be thrilling. Much depends on the severity of the

Finding open water in winter often yields nice sightings of waterfowl, like this Greater Scaup flock that also contains a Bufflehead and a male Canvasback, at the Philadelphia Naval Business Center.

cold and whether water remains ice-free, but generally this is a good month to see congregations of waterfowl and gulls. Some winters feature influxes of owls and finches. Keep a watchful eye on your bird feeders as cold concentrates birds where there is food, and unexpected visitors may appear, such as crossbills, redpolls, and others.

SITE	COUNTY	BIRDS
Middle Creek WMA	Lancaster	Geese and ducks
Presque Isle State Park	Erie	Ducks and gulls
Glen Ford on the Delaware	Philadelphia	Ducks and gulls

FEBRUARY Usually the coldest temperatures occur this month, and only the hardiest birds remain. Provided there is some ice-free water, February is a good time for waterfowl. Birds from arctic and sub-arctic areas may visit, such as owls and finches, and it is good time to search fields for open-country birds such as Snow Buntings and Lapland Longspurs.

SITE	COUNTY	BIRDS
FDR Park	Philadelphia	Ducks

| Amish Country | Lancaster/ Chester/ Mercer | Field birds |
| Point State Park | Allegheny | Gulls, waterfowl |

MARCH Signs of spring are in the air, though often winter still has a hold. Waterfowl and gulls are migrating, and large flocks of blackbirds are found feeding in fields and roosting in stands of trees.

SITE	COUNTY	BIRDS
Middle Creek WMA	Lancaster	Swans, geese
Presque Isle State Park	Erie	Ducks, gulls
Lake Somerset	Somerset	Ducks
Harvey's Lake	Luzerne	Ducks
Rushton Woods Preserve	Chester	American Woodcock
Tussey Mountain	Centre	Golden Eagle

APRIL Migration becomes more and more evident and the days get longer, activating hormones in birds that spur them to sing. Waterfowl numbers begin to dwindle, grebes appear, as herons, hawks, swallows, and sparrows increase. Always a sight for sore eyes, the hallmark birds of spring, warblers begin to appear.

SITE	COUNTY	BIRDS
Peace Valley Park	Bucks	Warblers, swallows, herons
Yellow Creek State Park	Indiana	Waterfowl, woodpeckers, warblers
Boyce-Mayview Park	Allegheny	Marsh birds
Beltzville State Park	Carbon	Waterfowl, swallows
Pymatuning-Conneaut Marsh	Crawford	Waterfowl

Spring creeps along until May when suddenly woodlands explode with sound and color. Birders wait all year for our forests to fill with warblers, like this Blackburnian Warbler.

MAY Perhaps the most thrilling month of the year for birding, May is an explosion of color and sound, and each and every day holds the fresh promise of newly arrived nesting birds and migrants. Birding can be great nearly anywhere, as warblers have stormed back, flycatchers return, sparrows are singing, and other stellar songbirds such as tanagers, grosbeaks, and cuckoos abound. Wetlands hold herons, rails, shorebirds, and other songbirds.

SITE	COUNTY	BIRDS
Frick Park	Allegheny	Migrant songbirds
John Heinz NWR	Philadelphia, Delaware	Herons, shorebirds, songbirds
Presque Isle State Park	Erie	Migrant songbirds, terns
Bald Eagle State Park	Centre	Songbirds, woodpeckers

JUNE Migration slows to a trickle, and basically ceases in mid June. Most birds have young or are tending nests. The vast and beautiful woodlands of Penn's Woods provide critical nesting habitat for many songbirds. June can be a good time also to visit grasslands where field birds nest.

SITE	COUNTY	BIRDS
Imperial Grasslands	Allegheny	Sparrows, field birds
Piney Tract	Clarion	Grassland birds
Delaware Water Gap NRA	Pike, et al.	Songbirds
Allegheny National Forest	Warren, et al.	Songbirds
Conneaut Marsh	Crawford	Marsh birds
Great Marsh	Chester	Marsh birds

Ruby-throated Hummingbirds nest throughout the state during the summer months, peaking in June and July. Males may take several partners during the season and will fiercely guard the "harem" in their territory.

JULY Summer temperatures soar and the breeding season is largely on the wane. Birdsong falls off as many young birds have fledged and are in (often confusingly drab) juvenile plumage. Many adult birds are molting and tend to be less conspicuous, as flying is laborious and risky as they replace their old and worn feathers. The first signs of autumn migration appear as shorebirds head south and herons wander away from usual breeding areas. Hotspots are similar to those in June and August.

SITE	COUNTY	BIRDS
Wildwood State Park	Dauphin	Herons
Lake Somerset	Somerset	Shorebirds, swallows

In summer the state's woodlands are spectacular for nesting songbirds, as are the rural areas and grasslands, and late in summer some wetlands attract gatherings of herons, such as the Great Blue Heron.

AUGUST As summer begins to fade, fall migration heats up and many warblers, swallows, terns, shorebirds, and herons are on the move.

October is a prime time to see migrating raptors, such as Cooper's Hawks, although some birds remain in Pennsylvania year-round.

SITE	COUNTY	BIRDS
Conejohela Flats	Lancaster	Herons, shorebirds
Green Lane Reservoir	Montgomery	Shorebirds, swallows
Coyler Lake	Centre	Shorebirds, swallows
Shenango Reservoir	Mercer	Shorebirds

SEPTEMBER   Large numbers of birds are heading south including warblers, flycatchers, cuckoos, grosbeaks and others, as well as shorebirds and hawks.

SITE	COUNTY	BIRDS
Fort Washington State Park	Montgomery	Hawks, songbirds
Peace Valley Park	Bucks	Hawks, songbirds
Yellow Creek SP	Indiana	Hawks, shorebirds, songbirds
Presque Isle SP	Erie	Songbirds

OCTOBER Just as in May and September, large numbers of birds are on the move, and nearly any patch of habitat can produce rewarding bird-watching. Cold fronts start to stack up more quickly, and hawkwatches attract crowds to witness spectacular raptor migrations. Some hawks begin moving in August, but activity peaks in October and continues to early December. Shorebirds and warblers dissipate, waterfowl numbers swell, and sparrows abound. Often the first signs of a winter finch invasion occur, with flyover flocks heard calling.

SITE	COUNTY	BIRDS
Hawk Mountain	Berks	Hawks
Waggoner's Gap	Perry	Hawks
Bake Oven Knob	Lehigh	Hawks
Pennypack on the Delaware	Philadelphia	Sparrows, finches

NOVEMBER Loons, grebes, and waterfowl become more and more apparent along lakes and rivers as they move south and away from the encroaching winter temperatures. Gull numbers rise and flocks begin to assemble along water bodies, and weedy fields and hedgerows may produce good sparrow sightings.

SITE	COUNTY	BIRDS
Allegheny Front	Bedford	Hawks, Golden Eagles
Hawk Mountain Sanctuary	Berks	Hawks, finches
Nockamixon State Park	Berks	Ducks, grebes, hawks

DECEMBER As the days grow short and the temperatures fall, winter begins in Pennsylvania, bringing more waterfowl. Fall migration is over early in the month, but as they try to settle in for the winter, birds are sometimes forced to move around by winter storms. The first good cold snaps may concentrate birds around water bodies, wastewater treatment plants and landfills, and anywhere that fruit or insects are concentrated.

SITE	COUNTY	BIRDS
Lake Somerset	Somerset	Waterfowl
Presque Isle SP	Erie	Waterfowl, loons, gulls
John Heinz NWR	Philadelphia	Waterfowl

Additional Resources

This book provides an overview of the common species in the state. For those interested in deepening their understanding of birds in the commonwealth, the following resources are recommended.

INTERNET RESOURCES

EBIRD (WWW.EBIRD.ORG)   A real-time online checklist and database for recording bird sightings, this dynamic project is rich in information and open to all. Exploring eBird, one will find maps of bird distribution, bar charts tracking bird abundance through the season -- all constructed through citizen science censuses. It is a great tool for learning about bird-watching areas near your home or at a travel destination, providing information about seasonal abundance of species.

ALL ABOUT BIRDS (WWW.ALLABOUTBIRDS.ORG)   An online bird guide to nearly 600 bird species found in the United States and Canada, with considerable information on behavior, natural history, and status and distribution.

XENO-CANTO (WWW.XENO-CANTO.ORG)   Studying and learning bird sounds is one of the fastest ways to improve understanding of birds. Learning bird sounds via print is difficult, but today there are many online resources useful for studying bird sounds. Xeno-canto is an internet archive of bird sounds from around the world. Listeners can explore a single species' sounds or an entire region's set of bird vocalizations.

PENNSYLVANIA ORNITHOLOGICAL RECORDS COMMITTEE (WWW.PABIRDS.ORG/RECORDS) Visit the PORC website for more information on the state's official bird list, including rare or seldom-seen species.

BOOKS In addition to general and comprehensive field guides to birds of North America, such as *The Sibley Guide to Birds*, Second Edition (Knopf, 2014) and the *Smithsonian Field Guide to Birds of North America* (HarperCollins, 2008), several excellent resources to Pennsylvania's birds are available including *The Birds of Pennsylvania* (Cornell University Press, 1999) and T*he Second Atlas of Breeding Birds in Pennsylvania* (Penn State University Press, 2012).

BIRD CLUBS If you find yourself looking for more information or are interested in finding other people who share your interest, consider joining a local, state or national bird club. Most clubs offer guided field trips. These are great social occasions, too. Nearly every county in the state hosts experts who take pride in sharing their knowledge and expertise. Such folks are often prominent in bird clubs, and being part of a bird club can offer all sorts of opportunities and access to useful information.

A good place to begin is the Pennsylvania Society for Ornithology (www.pabirds.org/). While a "society for ornithology" might sound rather austere and even intimidating, new members at meetings find themselves most welcome, and immediately part of a friendly and vibrant community. PSO welcomes novice birders and experts alike, and members receive the quarterly publication *Pennsylvania Birds*. The PSO website also hosts a page with a list of other local and regional bird clubs (www.pabirds.org/PABirdOrgs.htm).

The American Birding Association's mission is "to inspire people to protect and enjoy wild birds." ABA members receive publications such as *Birding* magazine, and have access to events, and membership dues support ABA conservation and community initiatives such as ABA Young Birder of the Year, Birding News, the ABA Blog, Birder's Exchange, the ABA Bird of the Year and more.

American Birding Association

Field Guide to Birds of Pennsylvania

Snow Goose

Chen caerulescens

L 30" | **WS** 54"

Flocks of this noisy goose are often heard before seen. Traveling groups chorus with high-pitched honks, mixed with hoarser grunts as they fly in loose wavy strings, shifting in shape. They seldom maintain an ordered "V" formation for long. Large numbers are seen in the Piedmont and along the coastal plain, but these geese are rare west of the Allegheny Front with the exception of Lake Erie. Most sightings in the state occur between October and April, more frequently during peak migration times in February and March, and then again in November and December. Snow Geese gather to feed and rest at farm fields, lakes, and rivers. Middle Creek WMA is a favored site, where numbers reach 50,000 or more. Because the geese root for plant matter in fields, many show brown or rust colored staining on the head.

White overall with black flight feathers.

Adult clean white; pink bill with blue "lipstick" is unique. Immature duskier gray and white, with darker bill.

Canada Goose

Branta canadensis

L 30–43" | **WS** 50–67"

One of the most familiar birds, this adaptable goose is a common statewide resident. Ambling around golf courses, farms, fields, city parks, ponds, and rivers, their honking *lunk* or *ha-lunk* call is heard year-round. Nearly any patch of water may host a pair. Canada Geese are aggressive in defending nest sites, even chasing people away at times. Migrant flocks are seen from February to March and October to December. Other smaller species and subspecies sometimes migrate in these flocks; most regular is the Cackling Goose (*Branta hutchinsii*), which is about half the size of a Canada Goose with a shorter neck.

Large goose with black head and neck, and white cheeks.

Strong fliers. Note black tail, white rump and undertail.

Mute Swan

Cygnus olor

L 60" | **WS** 75"

Native to Eurasia and popular among aviculturists, this swan is widely introduced in the U.S. and often regarded as a pest. It can be disruptive to native waterfowl in their brackish or freshwater habitats, and destructive to vegetation. Mute Swans occur in remote areas, but this is the only swan really at home in urban and suburban settings. Less social than our other large waterfowl, it is usually seen singly or in small family groups. Adults are easily identified; first-year birds are duskier, with darker bills. Adults defending nests can be aggressive toward people, even injuring them.

Very large. Adult white, with orange bill and black knob. Note long, pointed tail.

Juvenile dusky gray; lacks black knob on bill, and shows only a shadow pattern of adult bill pattern.

Tundra Swan

Cygnus columbianus

L 52" | **WS** 66"

Heard during fall migration, the pleasant, soft, mellow hooting of Tundra Swans is a sign of the onset of winter. Many migrate at night, calling hauntingly overhead. Typically they are seen in small flocks at lakes, rivers, and farm fields, and migrant flocks consist of close family groups. Fall migration peaks from November to December, and in the spring during March. Flocks of 1,000 or more individuals gather in winter at Middle Creek WMA, where they feed on tubers and other vegetation. In spring, flyover flocks occur widely, at times pausing at ponds or lakes. Rarely one or two Tundra Swans may summer somewhere in the state.

Adult white with black bill; variable yellow teardrop on bill. When feeding with head submerged, differs from Mute Swan in having a short tail.

Juvenile with dusky grayish head and gray upperparts. Bill mostly dark mixed with pink.

Wood Duck

Aix sponsa

L 20" | **WS** 27"

Wood Ducks are one of the most abundant breeding ducks in the state from October to May at beaver ponds, tree-lined lakes, creeks, old canals, and rivers. This duck nests in tree cavities up to 20 feet or more above the ground and will readily take to nest boxes. Dozens and even hundreds are seen at Heinz NWR in late summer and early autumn with smaller numbers present the rest of the year. Wood Ducks are vocal: males give a thin rising squeal; female's wailing call is often heard just as she takes flight. On flying birds, note the long tail, somewhat squared off at the tip.

Breeding males with red eye and bill, crazy crest, and white markings on the throat and flanks are gorgeous and unmistakable. In nonbreeding summer plumage, appear similar to females, but note red eye and bill.

Females are soft gray, sport a white eye patch, and a short crest. Dark bill, small white throat patch, and white stippling on chest and flanks.

Gadwall

Anas strepera

L 20" | **WS** 33"

This dabbling duck favors large lakes, ponds, slow-moving rivers, and marshy wetlands. Present in the state October through April, Gadwalls are absent from Pennsylvania during the warmer months. Like many migrant dabblers, it is especially common in the coastal plain and the Piedmont, but is local elsewhere. Gadwalls are most widespread as migrants in October and November, then again in early spring, and are mostly absent from the western half of the state in midwinter. Less obviously striking in plumage compared to many other ducks, the male Gadwall appears at close inspection to have beautiful and intricate patterns of black and white. Males emit an abrupt nasal *geek*, and females offer a simple *quack*.

Male marbled gray with black bill and black rear end from October to May. In nonbreeding plumage more similar to female.

Note mostly black bill with orange edges, round head, and white inner wing patch (speculum).

Northern Pintail

Anas acuta

L 25" | **WS** 34"

The pintail has a uniquely elegant shape. From mid-September to mid-April they are found nearly anywhere there is open water, but are most common in the southeastern Piedmont and coastal plain. Presque Isle and Yellow Creek State Parks, Middle Creek WMA, Heinz (Tinicum) NWR, and sites along the Allegheny and Susquehanna Rivers are good places to spot them. Spring migration peaks in March; the fall flight lasts from October to December. Pintails are less often heard than other dabbling ducks. Males give a high-pitched *preek*, often in rapid succession. Females give a quiet *quack*.

Long and slender with long neck and long tail. Breeding male (October to April) has brown head with white neck stripe. Bill black with blue-gray sides. Gray body, white belly, black undertail.

Female sandy brown, long neck and tail, dark bill.

American Wigeon

Anas americana

L 20" | **WS** 33"

Wary compared to other dabbling ducks, American Wigeons usually take to the air quickly at the approach of humans. The best time to see them is from September to April, especially when they are migrating in late February and March. Good sites include Yellow Creek State Park, Middle Creek WMA, Children's Lake, Lake Ontelaunee, and Heinz NWR. They frequent lakes, ponds, slow-flowing rivers, flooded fields, and marshy wetlands, and are usually in small flocks. More often than other dabbling ducks, they will mingle with diving ducks on deeper bodies of water, and sometimes keep company with American Coots. They eat plant matter and insects at the water's surface, and "up-end," raising their rear end and submerging the head and upper body to reach aquatic vegetation below. Wigeons are vocal, calling frequently. Males give a sneezy *whee whew;* females give a hoarse, coarse, low grunt, *herrnnh.*

Male has white crown, green eye stripe, peachy brown body, and pointed black tail. Bill is pale bluish with black border.

Female has small, round, speckled head. Bill pattern similar to male. In flight, both sexes show white shoulder patch.

American Black Duck

Anas rubripes

L 21-23" | **WS** 34.5-37.5"

With its understated dark plumage, the American Black Duck is often overlooked as it mingles with showier waterfowl. Though it frequently keeps company with Mallards, the Black Duck is less tolerant of people, often taking flight sooner and frequenting more secluded wetlands. Preferring wooded wetlands, marshes, slow-moving creeks or rivers, old canals, and lakes and ponds fringed by trees, it is widespread in Pennsylvania. Most abundant in winter and on migration from September through April, it is common in the southeast at sites including Middle Creek WMA, Green Lane Park, Heinz NWR, and the lower Susquehanna River. West of the Allegheny Front, good migration or wintering sites include Yellow Creek State Park, Whitetail Wetlands, and Pymatuning Reservoir. Black Ducks nest sparsely yet widely across the state. The largest numbers are in wooded wetlands of the Poconos.

Two American Black Ducks (rear) swim with a female Mallard (right front). Black Ducks are darker, gray-headed, and dark-tailed. Male with yellowish bill.

In both sexes, white underwings conspicuous in flight, as is a purplish blue speculum (rear wing patch).

Mallard
Anas platyrhynchos

L 22" | **WS** 34"

The Mallard is one of our most recognizable birds. The female Mallard's loud call, *quack!* causes the popular notion that ducks "quack." In fact, relatively few ducks "quack." Male Mallards offer a softer, coarse *weck, weck*. This is our most widespread duck species. Wild migrants breed here and visit from points to our north, and because the Mallard is popular with hunters and aviculturalists, we also have captive-reared birds that are released or escaped. As a result, Mallards may behave like wary wildfowl or like domesticated pets. They are at home in small urban duck ponds, large remote wetlands, and any water body in between.

Breeding plumage males with yellow bill, green head, white collar, gray body, and white tail. Note curled feathers at rump.

Female straw-brown with pale tail; orange bill with black in the middle. Males similar in appearance to females in summer.

Blue-winged Teal

Anas discors

L 15" | **WS** 23"

A small dabbling duck, the male Blue-winged Teal is beautifully spotted with a white half-moon on the face. Found on ponds, lakes, marshy areas, and flooded fields, this duck reveals its namesake blue wing patch in flight. It prefers shallow water, where it filters mud with its bill in search of invertebrates and seeds. A rare and opportunistic breeder in Pennsylvania, it is a regular migrant, with numbers peaking in April and again in September. It is sensitive to the cold, so it is rare in winter— absent from the west, but occasionally lingers in the southeast during mild winters. Look for it at Heinz NWR, Yellow Creek State Park, Lake Somerset, and other places where ducks congregate. Like other ducks, the Blue-winged Teal replaces its feathers in late summer, and during this period males resemble females. Despite being called a "teal," it is less closely related to the Green-winged Teal than to the Northern Shoveler, which also has a blue wing patch.

Breeding male is brown, speckled with black spots, with white crescent on face. Note white patch on rear flanks, bordering black undertail.

Female gray-brown with crisp pale fringes to body and back feathers. Note small size and dark bill that broadens at the sides toward the tip.

Note conspicuous blue wing patch in flight. Breeding males pictured here

Northern Shoveler

Anas clypeata

L 18" **|** **WS** 30"

The shoveler's bill gives this dabbling duck both its name and its unique appearance. The unusual bill is perfectly adapted to filter invertebrates and plants as shovelers swim low in the water. Shovelers are seen typically in small flocks, preferring shallow ponds, flooded fields, and marshy areas with emergent vegetation. Like other ducks, males and females pair on the wintering grounds, and shovelers remain paired longer than other ducks. They rarely breed in Pennsylvania but occur commonly as migrants in November and December and then in March. In winter they are scarce or locally common in ice-free areas near Lake Erie and in the southeast. Look for them at Heinz NWR, Lake Somerset, Conneaut Marsh, and Yellow Creek State Park.

Large spatulate bill broadens widely toward tip. Swimming males show much white on body and a chestnut flank patch. Note female's straw-colored plumage and heavy orange bill.

Male summer plumage is similar to female, but note his darker and less buffy head, duskier bill, and hints of chestnut and white on flanks.

In flight, look for blue "shoulders."

Green-winged Teal

Anas crecca

L 13" | **WS** 22"

These little ducks — smallest in North America — breed rarely in
Pennsylvania, and are generally absent in the state's plateau
region of the central-west and north. Otherwise, they appear fairly
widely from late August to May. Most often seen in migration, they
prefer marshy areas and shallow ponds but also stop on larger
water bodies where other waterfowl congregate. They sometimes
occur in flocks of dozens or even hundreds, especially in early
autumn when they mix with flocks of Blue-winged Teal. These
groups in August through October contain males and females, but
at this season males are largely brown, molting out of their
summer plumage, and appear similar to females. By the end of
October males have acquired breeding plumage and begin to
display for females. They call often, giving a shrill frog-like *creek*,
often repeated several times. The best months to see them are
March and April and from September to November. Good sites
include Presque Isle, Yellow Creek State Park, and the Susquehanna and Delaware Rivers.

Male from October to May has cinnamon
head, green eye stripe, marbled gray body,
and white stripe on side of breast.

Female similarly small; streaky brown overall with a dark bill. Also note distinctive wing pattern and cream-buff patch under the tail.

In flight the small size of this duck is quite apparent, due in part to its rapid, agile flight-style.

Lesser Scaup

Aythya affinis

L 17" | **WS** 29"

A widespread migrant and winter visitor, the Lesser Scaup occurs mostly from November through April. Usually on lakes and rivers, this diving duck also uses smaller ponds and wet marshy areas. Good sites include Yellow Creek State Park, Harvey's Lake, and Lake Erie where flocks of thousands are sometimes present. On large water bodies like Lake Erie and the Delaware River, Lesser Scaup mingle at times with the very similar Greater Scaup. Generally, the Lesser is more commonly encountered, and it is less comfortable in cold than the more northerly breeding Greater. During harsh winters flocks of Greater Scaup may contain single or small numbers of Lessers.

Mid-size diving duck with peaked crown, gray back, and paler gray flanks. Head shape is key in identifying scaup, but it can change shape depending on a bird's activity (Lesser's head may appear rounder when diving).

Female brown, with white feathering around base of bill. White around bill often seems dingier and less bright than Greater Scaup.

Greater Scaup

Aythya marila

L 19" | **WS** 30"

This robust diving duck with starkly contrasting plumage occurs in dozens to hundreds at Lake Erie and in smaller numbers along larger river such as the Allegheny, Susquehanna, and Delaware. Compared to other diving ducks, Greater Scaup prefer larger lakes and rivers where they dive for food, and are seldom seen on small patches of water. Absent in summer, they breed in Arctic and subarctic areas and migrate through Pennsylvania from October to April, with peak numbers in March, and often spend the winter.

Dark head, chest and rear end with pale gray back and white flanks. Similar to Lesser Scaup, but note rounded unpeaked head.

Female brown with relatively clean white patch around bill. Female similar to Lesser; note rounded head and broader bill. Many females show whitish around ear.

Redhead
Aythya americana

L 19" | **WS** 29"

With its subtle combination of colors, the male Redhead is easy on the eyes. Females are famous for laying their eggs in the nests of other ducks (called brood parasitism). Decades ago this species nested in Pennsylvania, but today it occurs only as a migrant and winter visitor. From November into April it shows up on deep lakes and large rivers, and is particularly numerous at the shore of Lake Erie. Numbers peak in March there, and this is also a good time to search for them at smaller water bodies around the state. Keep an eye out for Redheads along the Allegheny River near Kittanning, at Moraine State Park, Harvey's Lake, along the Lehigh and Susquehanna rivers, and along the lower Delaware River at sites like Pennypack and the Philadelphia Naval Business Center.

Mid-size diving duck; male has copper-red head, yellow eye, gray body, black chest. Bill is blue-gray with black tip.

Female has bulbous, rounded head, and gray-brown plumage. Note dark gray bill with black tip, and narrow white eye ring.

Canvasback
Aythya valisineria

L 21" | **WS** 33"

A handsome diving duck, the male Canvasback is distinctive. This and other dark-chested diving ducks including scaup, Ring-necked Duck, and Redhead are sometimes collectively called "pochards" or "bay ducks." The Canvasback does not breed in Pennsylvania, but occurs as a migrant and winters in a few places. Present from November into April, its numbers peak in February and March. Canvasbacks mostly frequent larger lakes and rivers, flocking with other diving ducks. At Lake Erie birders may see flocks of hundreds at Presque Isle, but the Canvasback is less regular and less numerous away from there. Good sites to check include larger rivers and lakes, such as Lake Somerset, the mouth of the Beaver River, and along the Delaware, Lehigh, and Susquehanna rivers. Lone birds are sporadically found on smaller lakes or ponds.

Elegant male is white-backed, with rusty chestnut head and long, sloping black bill.

Female similar in shape and general pattern, but lacks reddish tones and shows far less contrast, with tan-brown head and mottled gray back.

Ring-necked Duck

Aythya collaris

L 17" | **WS** 25"

Since the namesake feature is typically not visible, "Ring-necked" seems like an unusual common name. Males do have a chestnut ring around the neck, but this is a less useful field mark compared to the bird's noticeably peaked crown. Compared to the scaup and other diving ducks, the Ring-necked more often uses smaller freshwater bodies with tall emergent vegetation and trees. It occurs somewhat widely between October and April, but the migration peaks are in March and November. The largest numbers are on Lake Erie and along larger rivers and reservoirs of the Piedmont and coastal plain. When on larger lakes and rivers, they associate with other diving ducks, especially scaup.

Prominent white ring around bill. Dark chest and back, and pearly gray flank patch bordered by a vertical white stripe at the front.

Female is brownish with peaked crown, pale eye ring, and pale ring around the bill.

Surf Scoter

Melanitta perspicillata

L 23" | **WS** 30"

Nesting in the Arctic and wintering on the ocean, this sea duck is regular in Pennsylvania only along the shores of Lake Erie. It migrates in October and November and again in March and April. It is best sought out at Presque Isle during these periods. Even there and then, it is irregular in occurrence and usually in small numbers. Elsewhere in the state they are rare, but storms sometimes force them down onto lakes or rivers.

Adult males of this fairly large sea duck are known in coastal areas as "skunkheads" for their striking head pattern, with white nape patch. Note the heavy, colorful bill.

Females are brownish black, with a dark bill similar in shape to males'. Note smudgy white patches at base of bill and by the ear.

Black Scoter

Melanitta americana

L 19" | **WS** 33"

A rare visitor over most of Pennsylvania, the Black Scoter
breeds in the Artic and winters at sea, it is best sought during
fall migration at Lake Erie. From Presque Isle it is seen fairly
regularly, but its numbers vary from year to year, depending on
weather and other variables. Most are seen in November and
December, but this scoter also occurs in smaller numbers in
February and March. It is seen rarely elsewhere in the state
during those months, and occasionally storms force a flock
down onto a lake or river.

Males are jet black with sherbet-
orange bill patch. Round head and
relatively stubby bill are shaped
more like a dabbling duck than the
other scoters, which have longer
bills with sloping foreheads.

Female (front left) has gray cheeks that
contrast with a dark cap. In flight both
sexes show mostly grayish primaries.

White-winged Scoter
Melanitta fusca

L 21" | **WS** 31"

A hefty sea duck, the White-winged is more common away from the ocean than other scoters, and is regularly observed along the Lake Erie shore between late October and early April. Generally they prefer the deep water of large lakes and big rivers, but they occasionally turn up on smaller patches of water. More often they are seen in the western half of the state than the eastern, and they are less apt to mingle with other scoters. (Black and Surf Scoters readily flock with one another.) Since the 1980s non-native zebra mussels have proliferated in the Great Lakes, providing a new food source for the White-winged Scoter. Its numbers seem to be increasing, but when the lakes freeze, the scoters are forced to move south and may appear in a variety of locations.

Adult male is black overall, heavy, and long-bodied. Bill is long, sloping and with a reddish tip. Note the white teardrop around the eye. At rest, the white inner wing patch is not always visible, but it is striking when this duck takes flight.

Female and immature male are charcoal with white head patch at the ear and between eye and nostril. Note long, dark bill. White-winged is larger, heavier than Surf Scoter.

Long-tailed Duck

Clangula hyemalis

L 15-23" | **WS 28"**

The small, piebald Long-tailed Duck charms with its noisy disposition. Highly vocal, Long-taileds sound off repeatedly, giving an *onk-olawonk,* also transcribed as "south southerly" or "south south southerly." Long-tailed Ducks nest in the Arctic and winter on the ocean or the Great Lakes. In Pennsylvania they occur in unpredictable numbers at Lake Erie and on the larger rivers from late October to early April. Migrants may appear suddenly on large lakes and rivers during migration, and sometimes individuals or flocks are forced down by storms into smaller bodies of water. This is a strong-flying sea duck, capable of covering many miles. Flight is swift and buzzy, with rapid wingbeats.

Adult males are crisply marked in black and white with pink bill patch. Long tail feathers trail in the water and can be hard to see. In flight, short triangular wings are entirely black.

Female has smudgy black and white markings, mostly dark head and back, dark bill, white flanks, and lacks male's long tail.

Bufflehead
Bucephala albeola

L 14" | **WS** 21"

The stubby-billed, short-tailed, puffy-headed little Bufflehead is undeniably cute. It is the smallest diving duck, and its big round head seems too big for its tiny body. Its active diving behavior combined with its alert nature makes it all the more appealing. Absent in summer, it is widespread and common as a migrant, and is a regular winter visitor here from November through April. The largest numbers are seen in spring migration in March and April and in fall migration during November and December. Though numerous at Lake Erie and along the larger rivers, Buffleheads seldom form large flocks; they are more often seen singly or in small groups.

Small, active diving duck, with big white head patch and extensive white below. When distant, appears mostly white. Bill is dark grayish.

Females are mostly dusky blackish gray or charcoal, with white ear patch and black bill. In flight note the small whitish belly patch and small white inner wing patch (the speculum).

Common Goldeneye

Bucephala clangula

L 18" | **WS** 32"

The stocky, big-headed goldeneye is a hardy, lively diving duck at home during the cold Pennsylvania winter. Usually it is the last of the winter waterfowl to show up in late November or December, staying north as far as there is ice-free water. During winters where waters to our north freeze over, larger numbers move south into the state. They arrive in small flocks, remaining until late March or early April on lakes, rivers, and ponds, where they dive for small fish and aquatic invertebrates. At the shore of Presque Isle large numbers are seen, especially in March. Away from Lake Erie they occur along larger rivers and lakes, but are more sparsely distributed and in smaller numbers. Look for them at Pymatuning Reservoir, Merrill Creek Reservoir, the Susquehanna River, Morrisville Levee, and elsewhere along the Delaware River.

Male black and white, mostly dark head and mostly white body. Long bill and big, angular head with round white cheek spot.

Female also has golden eye, but is gray with an angular brown head. Bill is dark and may show orangish at tip.

Common Merganser
Mergus merganser

L 24" | **WS** 33"

Widespread in winter and on migration at lakes, rivers, and ponds, Common Mergansers are pursuit-divers that use the strong legs and feet to propel their streamlined bodies through the water after fish. At the surface they appear long-bodied, and the male's white plumage is apparent even at great distances. Close up, lucky observers may notice the bill has saw-like serrations, useful for snagging prey, which is why they are called "sawbills" in some localities. Numbers are greatest from December into April, and large incursions associated with cold fronts occur when birds are "iced out" of areas farther north. Common Mergansers nest in Pennsylvania along wooded creeks and rivers with good-quality clear water. They fly strongly with rapid, stiff wingbeats.

Largest merganser; male mostly white-bodied; dark, rounded head has a greenish sheen. Red bill.

Female shows a clean divide between the gray body and brown head.

Red-breasted Merganser

Mergus serrator

L 22" | **WS** 27"

With a spiky, unkempt crest, and a skinny neck, the wild-eyed
Red-breasted Merganser is both beautiful and odd-looking. Long
and slender, like other mergansers it preys on fish and aquatic
invertebrates, diving frequently. Usually observed swimming low
in the water, it often keeps to the more sheltered parts of large
lakes or broad slow-moving rivers. Best seen at Lake Erie from
November into May, where counts over 10,000 are sometimes
tallied at Presque Isle. Away from there it is unpredictable, less
numerous, and generally uncommon. Keep an eye out for it at
Moraine State Park, Bald Eagle State Park, the mouth of the
Beaver River, and along the Susquehanna and Delaware rivers,
near the offshoot of a tributary. They migrate along rivers and are
seen occasionally over hawkwatches.

Male has spiky crest, white collar, and
black-speckled rusty breast. Female and
young males similar with wispy crest and
showing little contrast between cinnamon
head and brownish gray body.

Hooded Merganser
Lophodytes cucullatus

L 17" | **WS** 25"

The spectacular Hooded Merganser with its "hairy" head and elegant markings ranks among the most eye-catching of our ducks. When pairing up in winter males display for females by throwing back their heads and sounding off with a reedy, frog-like *Pah-Whaaaaaaaa!* Breeding at scattered sites around the state, particularly in the northwest, it nests in tree cavities by still, clear water. Most people see Hooded Mergansers as migrants and winter visitors from November through April, when they occur in pairs or small flocks. They frequent a variety of wetland habitats, and good sites include Pymatuning Reservoir, Harvey's Lake, Bald Eagle SP, Beltzville State Park, and Lake Ontelaunee.

Male has white crest edged with black; flanks chestnut.

Similar size and tubular shape as male, but female is uniform brown with a shaggy brown crest.

Ruddy Duck

Oxyura jamaicensis

L 15" | **WS** 23"

Shaped like a rubber-ducky, the stiff-tailed broad-billed Ruddy
Duck is one charismatic little duck. Compact, tubby, and buoyant,
they swim about in tight groups on ponds and lakes, with their
tails cocked up, and are sometimes seen along wide rivers. They
feed on invertebrates during the day and night. Look for them at
Yellow Creek State Park, Rose Valley Lake, Harvey's Lake,
Chambers Lake, and Moraine State Park. Observed in Pennsylvania mostly from October into May, the Ruddy Duck is unusual
among ducks in that it acquires its breeding plumage in spring.
Most ducks pair in winter, entering breeding plumage in autumn.

Most of the year, Ruddy Ducks are
grayish brown with whitish cheeks,
dark crowns, and gray-brown bodies.
Breeding males turn ruddy brown
and sport a bright blue bill.

Female dusky gray-brown overall,
with dark bill, pale belly, dark
stripe through the pale cheeks.

Northern Bobwhite

Colinus virginianus

L 10" | **WS** 13"

Heard much more often than seen, this handsome, vocal quail is named for its call. The exclamatory "Bob-white!" is heard much less often today than it was a few decades ago. Due to changes in farming practices and other land uses, this popular gamebird has declined by over 80 percent in the southern half of the state, where it was once common. This, combined with a long history of releases of captive-reared birds for hunting, has clouded the bird's status today, and there are no known viable breeding populations left in the state. Most seen now are likely released pen-reared birds. Bobwhites prefer dense grassy areas, overgrown agricultural fields, thickets, openings in scrub barrens, burned over areas, and scrubby hedgerows. Since they are intolerant of snow cover, they are not encountered in the mountains and plateaus, but they are still occasionally found along the Piedmont in the south-central part of the state.

Male has white cheeks and a white eyebrow. Black stripe behind eye curves down to the throat. Brown body is spotted white below.

Female is similar to male, but less contrasting in plumage with buffy throat and eyebrow.

Ring-necked Pheasant

Phasianus colchicus

L 24" | **WS** 28"

The Ring-necked Pheasant is a Eurasian native, but in the U.S. it is commonly reared in captivity and released for sport. It is resident statewide in grassy fields, farmlands, along open roadsides, in overgrown brushy areas, and at the edge of woodlands. A nimble runner, it prefers to trot away from people rather than fly, but when flushed, it explodes loudly into the air with loud wingbeats. Though occasionally seen in small flocks, usually a pheasant is alone or a male is seen with a female. Males vocalize especially at dawn with a harsh, grating *cronk-cronh* that attracts females and alerts other males that the territory is occupied.

Large, long-tailed gamebird with terrestrial habits. Male unmistakable with red face, white collar, and ornate copper-bronze plumage.

Female straw-brown with pointed tail, and pale whitish teardrop-like mark at the eye.

Ruffed Grouse

Bonasa umbellus

L 16-20" | **WS** 20-25"

Appropriately, this is the state bird of "Penn's Woods." At first glance it may appear only as a brown chicken-like bird, but a closer look reveals gorgeous plumage with fine barring and marbling. The male engages in a dramatic display called "drumming," in which he fluffs out his black neck feathers and pumps his wings, making a thumping sound that can be heard from quite a distance, and resonates in your chest when the bird is close. Absent from lower Piedmont, the coastal plain, and much of the southwest, the grouse is a widespread resident in the upper Piedmont, the mountains, and across the central and northern counties. Usually seen singly and on the ground, it is occasionally spotted in trees and shrubs foraging for wild fruits and berries. Preferring remote woodlands, the grouse likes open thickets amid expansive forested areas and often resides in younger forests with good regenerating stem growth.

Short-crested, with intricate patterning, including black on sides of neck, thin white eye line, black and white scalloping along flanks, and black tail band. Some individuals reddish brown; others gray.

Wild Turkey

Meleagris gallopavo

L 42" | **WS** 53"

The Wild Turkey is rather comical in comportment but also beautiful, sporting colorful green and rusty markings. Perhaps more common in Pennsylvania now than in the pre-Colonial era, turkeys are found throughout the state year-round. Like other game birds, it is most conspicuous in spring, when small or medium-size groups are seen; males fluff themselves up into a ball, jack up their tails, and stride about. Every so often the male gives a descending loud gobble, which can be heard at a distance. Turkeys frequent wooded areas near fields, where they slowly walk and peck at the ground, hunting for fruit, seeds, and insects. Benjamin Franklin wrote to his daughter in 1784 suggesting that the Wild Turkey, and not the Bald Eagle, would be a more appropriate as the national symbol, "The Turkey is in Comparison a much more respectable Bird, and withal a true original Native of America...He is besides, though a little vain & silly, a Bird of Courage."

Female usually lacks tufts present on male's chest, and has a less colorful head.

Displaying males puff out their feathers dramatically. Note breast tuft and pale tail band. Red wattle hangs over the dark bill. Rump is rusty brown.

Red-throated Loon

Gavia stellata

L 24" | **WS** 43"

Nesting in the Arctic, the Red-throated Loon is the smaller of the two loons that occur in Pennsylvania, where it is a scarce migrant and rare winter visitor. Migration peaks in March and April and again in November, and in winter it is sometimes seen on larger lakes and rivers on the coastal plain and Piedmont. It is best sought at Presque Isle, along the Delaware River, the Susquehanna River, at Rose Valley Lake, and is occasionally seen as a flyover at hawk migration sites. Seldom seen in breeding plumage in Pennsylvania, nearly all are adults in their black and white winter plumage, or are gray-plumaged juveniles.

Winter adults and juveniles lack red throat patch. Note slender shape, slightly upturned thin bill, and extensively white face.

Common Loon

Gavia immer

L 31" | **WS** 46"

A signature species of northern lakes in the U.S. and Canada, the Common Loon is famous for its ethereal wails and tremolos. It is most frequently seen in Pennsylvania while in winter or juvenile plumage. The chunky, block-headed Common Loon occurs here mostly as a migrant from October through December and in spring from March into May. It is also found in winter in smaller numbers, where lakes and rivers remain ice-free. Awkward on land, it swims gracefully, usually staying low in the water, except when preening. Diving for fish, a loon can remain underwater for over a minute or more before resurfacing, sometimes quite a distance away. Observed flying high over hawk watches, the Common Loon has powerful wingbeats and looks well balanced, as its feet seem about the same size as its head. Like other migrant waterbirds, loons are occasionally grounded by storms.

Breeding adult jet black, spotted white on back. Note sharp black bill and white collar, breast, and underparts.

Winter adult and juvenile blackish above and white below. Note large size, big blocky head, heavy bill, and partial neck collar.

Loons are large birds and need a long "airstrip" to take off from the water's surface. Once in flight, they are powerful and long distance fliers with some migrating hundreds of miles per day.

Pied-billed Grebe

Podilymbus podiceps

L 13.5" | **WS** 21"

The pudgy Pied-billed Grebe swims at the edges of ponds, lakes, and marshes, surfacing quietly before diving again for food. Eating fish, crustaceans, and invertebrates, it is hardly ever seen out of the water. Sightings usually are of lone individuals, but sometimes several work the same patch of water. Named for the striking pattern on the bill during the breeding season, it breeds sparingly across the state, making nests in larger marshes. As nesting approaches, they become vocal in April and May, giving a loud series of whooping *whoo whoo whoo* calls, or a rapid rattling series of *kip, kip'em* calls. Often when sounding off, they are hard to see amid dense wetland vegetation. Generally this grebe is secretive in summer; more are seen from September through April, when they occupy open water.

Small with a bulbous head, and almost no tail. Brown overall, breeding adults have white bill with vertical black stripe, and black throat.

Nonbreeding birds have dusky beige bill, and a paler head and also show unkempt white rear-end.

Nests are on floating mats of vegetation. Tiny chicks are striped black and white.

Horned Grebe

Podiceps auritus

L 13" | **ws** 23.5"

The small, red-eyed Horned Grebe might seem misnamed at first. Most Pennsylvania birds are in black-and-white winter plumage, lacking the buffy tufts ("horns") on the head. Bright breeding plumage begins to appear during spring migration. Absent here in summer, this small diving waterbird occurs in winter, but is seen mostly during migration in March and April or in fall in November and December. After storms, Horned Grebes may appear suddenly and in numbers, when wind and precipitation force them out of the sky and into the nearest water body. Like other grebes, the Horned Grebe seems intermediate between a duck and a loon in appearance and behavior, swimming and diving at large open ponds, lakes and rivers. Good spots to search for them include Presque Isle, Shawnee, Yellow Creek, and Beltzville State Parks, Rose Valley Lake, and along the major rivers.

In breeding plumage, dark upperparts, buffy eyebrows, cinnamon underparts.

In nonbreeding plumage, dark cap, blackish upperparts, white throat and cheeks, and paler flanks. Pale bluish gray bill is thin and straight.

Red-necked Grebe

Podiceps grisegena

L 17-22" | **WS** 24-27"

The Red-necked Grebe is a rare and unpredictable migrant and winter visitor in Pennsylvania, occurring from November to April. It is most reliably seen is at Lake Erie during migration. Migration flights peak between mid-October and mid-December, and in spring in March and April. Occasionally, sudden winter cold snaps freeze water bodies to our north and push many grebes south to Pennsylvania lakes and rivers. This species prefers deeper water than other grebes. The red neck is acquired during breeding season in late March or April well after most of these grebes have left for nesting areas to our north.

Large grebe with long neck and heavy, pointed bill. Breeding adults distinctive with red neck, silver cheeks, black cap.

Nonbreeding adults and juveniles less neatly patterned, less colorful, generally dusky gray-brown. Note long yellowish bill, grayish cheeks, dark cap. In flight, wings show white patches along shoulders and secondaries.

Double-crested Cormorant

Phalacrocorax auritus

L 31.5" | **WS** 46.5"

A prehistoric-looking waterbird lacking showy plumage or ornamentation, the Double-crested Cormorant is often overlooked. Common in the state and frequenting almost any patch of water, it is seen swimming in search of fish, or perched on a snag or post, and often basking in the sun with its wings held aloft. Its population has surged in recent decades and now large flocks gather along lakes and large rivers. Seasonally their numbers remain stable through most of the year, but cold winters with freezing temperatures force them away in search of open water. In flight they appear goose-like, but with shorter, thicker necks. Flocks fly in loose lines or "V" formations. The namesake black crests are apparent only in spring and summer and at close range.

Adults black overall with yellow-orange throat and mandible.

Immatures are browner than adults, with pale brownish breast and neck.

Great Cormorant

Phalacrocorax carbo

L 33–25" | **WS** 51–63"

The Great Cormorant is mainly a marine species, and in Pennsylvania it occurs only along the lower Delaware River and rarely along the lower Susquehanna River. Nesting along the Atlantic coast of Canada, it is a winter visitor here from October into April. The Great Cormorant likes to sit up high, preferring prominent perches such as channel markers, pilings, and other man-made structures. Seeing solitary cormorants is not uncommon, but in some places they gather to hunt for fish, or to roost. In these situations, they will mingle with the smaller Double-crested, which usually outnumber them. Look for Great at the Philadelphia Naval Business Center, Pennypack on the Delaware, and other Delaware River viewpoints south of Levittown.

Note large size, blocky head, heavy bill. Adult black with white chin. Breeding adults have white patches on rear flanks.

Immatures have pale whitish belly and dark breast, the opposite pattern of immature Double-crested.

American Bittern

Botaurus lentiginosus

L 28.5" | **WS** 36"

This heron's popularity is reflected in its many local names, such as "bog bull," "star-gazer," "thunder-pumper," and "stake-driver." The latter two names refer to its unusual deep *glunk-a' lunk* or "plum-puddin" call during the breeding season. The American Bittern breeds in small numbers at large freshwater marshes with extensive stands of cattails. Although it occurs only sparsely, it may be found all year. It is most often detected as a migrant in April and then in October and November. Secretive, it usually stays hidden amid dense marsh vegetation, moving slowly and deliberately often with its bill pointing up. Look for this bittern at Heinz NWR or at the large marshes in Crawford and Tioga counties.

Mid-size, brown overall, and beautifully marked in golden or bronze; bold neck stripes; white throat. In flight it shows blackish wings. Note the dark brown or blackish stripe on sides of neck.

Least Bittern

Ixobrychus exilis

L 12" | **WS** 16"

The diminutive Least Bittern is our smallest and most secretive heron. Mostly nocturnal, staying always within dense marsh vegetation, such as cattails, sedges, and occasionally spatterdock, it is seldom seen. Tiny as it is, and moving deliberately when active during the day, it is hard to spot and always a lucky find. Occasionally one surprises birders by flying by in broad daylight, but more often it moves in and out of sight along marsh edges, often grasping emergent and woody vegetation with its feet as it stalks its prey. Unlike other herons, the Least Bittern is more easily heard than seen, and it is often heard at night, dawn, or dusk, giving a steady, hoarse, frog-like *goo, goo, goo, goo* or *cuc cuc cuc*. Absent in winter, it is seen here from May to September, and nests in small numbers at wetlands in Philadelphia, Crawford, and Erie counties, and spottily elsewhere.

Tiny, with strikingly buffy plumage. Adult males have black back and cap.

Females are paler buff with brownish cap. Note distinct white lines on neck and shoulder, and contrast between wings and back.

Great Blue Heron

Ardea herodias

L 38-54" | **WS** 66-79"

The most commonly encountered heron in the state, the Great Blue's very large size, tall stature, and gray upperparts are familiar to birdwatchers. It appears dignified until you hear it call, then it's easy to know why it is sometimes known as "old cranky." The call is a series of abrupt and dissatisfied, harsh croaks, *Crack! Rack raaap.* They take a variety of foods, not limited to fish, but also to birds, frogs, reptiles, and even rodents as large as muskrats! Nearly any body of water at any season may harbor a Great Blue, or several, and they breed widely in small or moderate-size colonies. When flying to and from colonies or evening roosts, the Great Blue appears heavy and slow, with deliberate wingbeats.

Large, tall heron, gray overall (more gray than blue) with long neck and legs. White face and central crown, with black eye stripe. Immature duskier, especially along neck and face, and has a dark cap.

In flight, curls the neck inward and trails the legs behind, making it look front-heavy.

Great Egret

Ardea alba

L 40" | **WS** 54"

The Great Egret is eye-catching as it stalks fish at the edges of
wetlands, marshes, and other water bodies. This is our most
widespread white heron, but like most wetland birds it is largely
absent in heavily wooded central and northern areas. It is common
from April through October in many areas. Breeding occurs at a
couple of sites on the Susquehanna, including Wade Island and
Kiwanis Lake Park. As the breeding season comes to a close in
August and September, numbers swell and aggregations gather at
wetlands and marshes, especially in the southeast and Crawford
County. In winter its numbers decrease, but occasionally a few
persist into January in the southeast, such as at Heinz NWR.

Large heron, with elegant
stature, tall and white.
Note the yellow-orange
bill and black legs.

Snowy Egret

Egretta thula

L 24" | **WS** 39"

The dapper, medium-size Snowy Egret occurs here, usually in small numbers, from April through September. Mostly it is an uncommon bird, occurring mainly in the southeast, and is rare west of the Allegheny Front. It is seen with some regularity along the lower Delaware River and along the Susquehanna River, especially in August and September. Snowy Egrets favor shallow water in marshes or at the edges of pools, ponds, lakes, or rivers. Compared to the larger, more deliberate Great Egret, the Snowy Egret hunts more actively, running and darting around, and making short flights. But sometimes it will hold a waterside vigil, standing still and patiently waiting for a fish to come close before stabbing at it.

Mid-size heron, with a slender black bill. Adults have black legs with yellow feet. In spring breeding plumage, note a short bushy crest, and fan-like plumes coming off the back. Juveniles have greenish legs.

Little Blue Heron
Egretta caerulea

L 24" | **WS** 40"

A slow-moving heron, rare in Pennsylvania, the Little Blue strides deliberately along the edges of pools, ponds, lakes, and slow flowing river. It stops at times, seemingly frozen in place while it waits to nab a fish, crab, or frog. Often it is solitary, but sometimes is attracted to areas where other herons gather. Little Blues are found mainly in the southeastern Piedmont and coastal plain between April and October. Search for it especially in late summer, along the Susquehanna River, including Conejohela Flats and river islands, and at John Heinz NWR. It is much rarer west of the Allegheny Front, but occasionally one is seen at a wetland along the western edge of state from Erie to Pittsburgh.

Adults are inky blue with a purplish head, and thick, two-toned bill. Juvenile (inset) white overall with yellow legs.

Black-crowned Night-Heron
Nycticorax nycticorax

L 24" | **WS** 45.5"

This heron, as its name implies, is most active at night. At dusk and dawn, it gives a loud *wok!* when taking flight to move between resting spots and feeding areas. The short, thick, pointed bill is useful for snatching a great variety of prey, including fish, worms, and insects. Sometimes night-herons feed during the day, but usually they conceal themselves under the canopy of a tree or within thick bushes and shrubs, usually in small groups called roosts. It occurs mainly from April through October, and nests along the Susquehanna River and locally elsewhere in the Piedmont. This species occurs mostly in the state's southeastern area. Absent from the plateau, this bird occurs mostly in the southeast, but is occasionally seen along the western border from Pittsburgh to Erie.

Stocky with short legs, big head, and short, thick, pointed bill. Adult is pearl gray with black back and crown. Immature brown, spotted white with yellowish bill and legs.

Yellow-crowned Night-Heron

Nyctanassa violacea

L 24" **WS** 42"

One of the state's rarest breeding birds, this night-heron nests in only a few places along the Susquehanna River, in and around Harrisburg. A few pairs nest elsewhere nearby, but away from this section of the Susquehanna it is rare. It occurs here from April through October, mostly near the nesting colonies, or as a migrant along the coastal plain. It is classified as Endangered in the state. In other areas the Yellow-crowned Night-Heron eats crabs, but it has also been observed eating insects, worms, and crayfish including the invasive rusty crayfish.

Immature dark gray with dark bill.

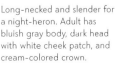

Long-necked and slender for a night-heron. Adult has bluish gray body, dark head with white cheek patch, and cream-colored crown.

Green Heron

Butorides virescens

L 17" | **WS** 26"

From late April to mid-October, the small Green Heron is wide-spread and common, breeding in most of the state. Nesting in trees near marshes, in swampy woodlands, and along forested rivers, it occurs in other wetland habitats, especially during migration. Its solitary nature and habit of foraging in wooded areas set it apart from our other common herons. A Green Heron is usually spotted sitting inconspicuously and still at the water's edge, where it moves slowly with deliberate stretching steps, raising its crown and tail feathers according to its mood. Periodically it stabs at a fish with its long, slender bill. When it takes to the air, it gives a loud, startling *kieu! kyow, kyow* or *kuk kuk*.

Short and squat, with dark, straight bill, dark green cap, green back, chestnut neck, and white stripe down center of throat.

Glossy Ibis
Plegadis falcinellus

L 23" | **WS** 36"

Given its steeply curved bill, long neck, slender body, and long legs, few birds are as distinctive in shape as the Glossy Ibis. A wading bird, the ibis works marshes, ponds, flooded fields, and wet meadows, walking in shallow water or wet muddy areas, unearthing invertebrates. It is uncommon to rare in Pennsylvania with most sightings from the southeast between April and September. It breeds along the coast, and most sightings here are of spring migrants in April or May, or in late summer after the breeding season. Sometimes single birds are sighted, but occasionally they occur in small flocks. Flying flocks of distant ibis can be hard to distinguish from cormorants, but ibis flocks are more haphazard in the air, with faster and more erratic wing beats. Keep an eye out for them along the Susquehanna River, especially near the Conejohela Flats, and along the lower Delaware River, especially at Heinz NWR.

Fairly large, and dark overall with long bill curved downward. Adults show iridescence in wings and tail. Breeding adults have pale bluish white lines between eye and bill.

Black Vulture

Coragyps atratus

L 25" | **WS** 59"

A stocky vulture with a short tail and a dark head, the Black
Vulture is usually seen circling over open areas and farm country.
It patrols country roads and highways for roadkills, often associating with Turkey Vultures, which have a much keener sense of
smell and can lead the Black Vulture to a carcass. It also forages in
garbage at landfills, and roosts on dead snags, or tall towers. It is
common throughout the mountains and valleys, the Piedmont and
coastal plain, but is rarer west of the Allegheny Front. An
increasing visitor in the state and a breeder in the Piedmont, a few
decades ago this species was uncommon in Pennsylvania. Its
higher numbers today probably result from an increase in deer,
combined with an increase in vehicle traffic that produces more
roadkills for food.

Dark head and bill with gray bill
tip. In flight (inset), note short
tail, broad wings, and white
"hands" at wing tips; flight is a
quick series of shuffling flaps,
mixed with longer glides.

Turkey Vulture
Cathartes aura

L 41" | **WS** 68.5"

A famous scavenger of roadkill, the brown and black Turkey Vulture uses its powerful sense of smell (uncommon in birds) to locate food. It careens along roadsides, gliding while holding its wings in a "V", and teeters back and forth, rocking gently and seldom needing to flap. Given the large size and impressive wingspan, this bird is often misidentified as a hawk or an eagle. While many birds use sound to attract a mate, vultures hardly vocalize, and only occasionally give a hiss. Often referred to as a "buzzard," this vulture is found throughout the state all year, yet some populations are migratory, heading for Florida, the Gulf Coast, and Central and South America for the winter.

Adult has bare red head, with a white tip to bill. Note brownish back. At rest, long wings and tail make the rear end seem long.

In flight, note teetering and gliding, small head, and silvery wings held in a "V."

Osprey
Pandion haliaetus

L 22" | **WS** 64"

From March through October the popular and widespread "fish hawk" hunts waters nearly statewide. Sitting atop dead snags and other prominent perches, the Osprey circles around lakes and rivers, every so often swooping down and diving into the water to snag a fish. Sometimes an Osprey will circle high with a fish it has caught, vocalizing loudly, which may attract the attention of an eagle. Bald Eagles will chase down and overtake Ospreys stealing their catch. With its large size and mostly white head, casual observers confuse Ospreys with the Bald Eagle, and the two often occur together. Both raptors like rivers and lakes, but the Osprey is smaller and flies with its wings crooked slightly back. Ospreys nest mostly at still water rather than flowing water in Pennsylvania and often nest on artificial structures. Many migrate to South America for winter, and large numbers are tallied at hawk-watching sites, rivers, and lakes during peak migration in April and September.

Large, with white chest and dark brown back. Mostly white head shows dark line through eye.

Golden Eagle

Aquila chrysaetos

L 30" | **WS** 80"

The Golden Eagle is a fierce and regal raptor. Mostly it hunts rabbits and rodents, larger birds, and sometimes scavenges for food. In other parts of its range this remarkable bird of prey is known to have taken animals as large as pronghorns and mountain goats, and it can defend its kills from bears and coyotes. Relatively rare in Pennsylvania, it is found here from October to April, and most are seen as migrants at hawk-watching sites along ridges such as at Tussey Mountain (where March is best) and from mid-October into early December at sites such as Hawk Mountain and the Allegheny Front. It is rare away from the mountains and is generally scarce in winter, but it may turn up almost anywhere in the state.

Dark brown adult has buffy undertail coverts and gold on head and neck. When soaring, wings are held in a slight "V."

Bald Eagle
Haliaeetus leucocephalus

L 33" | **WS** 80"

Our cherished national bird is conspicuous and widespread in
Pennsylvania today. A remarkable conservation success story,
back in the 1980s the state had just a couple of pairs in
Crawford County. Now Bald Eagles nest widely, even in
Philadelphia at Heinz NWR and Pennypack on the Delaware
River. The symbolic raptor is a regular breeding bird farther
north on the Delaware and along the Susquehanna River, and
breeds commonly around lakes and wetlands in the northwest.
When nesting, it eats mostly fish and is nearly always near
water, but at other seasons it hunts birds and animals, and
scavenges food. Many are seen at autumn hawk-watches, when
the Bald Eagle is one of the first raptors of the season to start
moving. Adults migrate in September, and youngsters have a
more protracted migration. In winter, eagles may gather in
roosts (sometimes dozens) along the lower Susquehanna and
Delaware Rivers, and in the Pymatuning area. They vocalize
fairly frequently while in the air, giving a surprisingly weak
series of piping chirps.

Massive bird of prey, adults have
white head and tail, brown body
and large yellow bill.

Eagles take about four years to become white-headed adults Juveniles and immatures are dark chocolate brown overall with white "wingpits." Second year birds are mottled brown and white below.

Huge wingspan; wings rectangular with long "fingers" at end.

Northern Harrier

Circus cyaneus

L 19" | **WS** 43"

Flying low over marshes, grasslands and farm fields, the harrier looks to surprise prey, including small birds and rodents. Its wide owl-like facial discs direct sounds to the ears helping it to detect rustling movements of mice and other small mammals. It is a scarce breeding bird at scattered sites across the state, more often seen from September into April. It nests mostly in grasslands and larger wetlands, especially at higher elevations and in northern counties. As a winter visitor and a migrant, it may occur almost anywhere, but it is best sought in large fields, reclaimed strip mines, and at hawk migration sites in the mountains such as Waggoner's Gap, Hawk Mountain, Stone Mountain Hawkwatch, and Tuscarora Summit.

Note long wings and tail, and a conspicuous white rump. Males are sometimes called "gray ghosts"; some are brownish gray, others pale gray. Harriers teeter in flight.

Females and juveniles are brown with a white rump. Juveniles (pictured) have buffy chest. Females are pale below but have brown streaking.

Broad-winged Hawk

Buteo platypterus

L 15" | **WS** 34"

Gliding with tapered, pointed wings and a short tail, the Broad-winged Hawk is seen at times by the hundreds, as it passes fall hawk-watching sites along the ridges and Piedmont, headed for South America. Spending the winter in the tropics, the Broad-winged returns in April migrating northward and breeding in much of the state. The massive fall migration passes along the ridges and in the southeast during mid-September, when flocks assemble in "kettles," swirling groups of hawks that circle together. On certain days spectacular flights of hundreds or even thousands are seen at hawk-watching sites such as Militia Hill and Hawk Mountain. It is much less conspicuous when breeding. The Broad-winged nests and hunts within (or at the edge of) the forest, and though it moves hundreds of miles during migration, once it is on a summer territory, it seldom is far from its nest.

Adult brown above with brown barring on breast and short, banded tail. Underwings pale, with dark trailing border.

Juvenile similar to juvenile Red-shouldered, but averages paler below and darker above. Secondaries are solid brown, and in flight the wings lack pale crescents.

Cooper's Hawk

Accipiter cooperii

L 15" | **WS** 30"

The Cooper's Hawk is probably our most commonly encountered raptor after the Red-tailed Hawk. Widespread across the state, the Cooper's population has increased substantially in recent decades, as it has adapted well to suburban and urban landscapes. Studies suggest that it may actually be more numerous in such areas than in natural landscapes. Alert and agile, it perches often mid-story in a tree and then surprises pigeons and other birds, nimbly pursuing prey into and through the woods. Most often seen in flight, Cooper's may give away its presence vocally, giving *kek kek kek kek* calls that may get louder as they progress, and a *whee-er* sound, similar to a sapsucker's call.

Large with a round head, a blue cap and a paler nape. Adults bluish gray above, reddish below. Often shows a crisp whitish band at the tail tip.

Immatures streaked brown below, with pale undertail and brown back. In flight, as with adults, note rounded tail with thin white band. Unlike Sharp-shinned, the large head projects in front of its wings.

Sharp-shinned Hawk

Accipiter striatus

L 11.5″ | **WS** 19″

A small songbird-hunting raptor, the Sharp-shinned Hawk is a serious little predator. It is famous for staking out bird feeders, which attract its prey. It is at times first detected while perched in a tree, but most often it is seen in the air. Like a smaller, more compact version of the more widely encountered Cooper's Hawk, when the Sharpie takes flight it intersperses quick wingbeats with longer glides. When gliding or soaring, the shoulders and wrists of the wing are pushed forward and held near the head. It is widespread throughout the state over most of the year, but is best seen during migration at hawk-watching sites in September and October. It is less conspicuous in summer when nesting, preferring more forested areas than the Cooper's Hawk, and often is associated with evergreen conifers.

Adults have blue-gray back and cap; chest is barred reddish. Females average larger than males, and confusing female Sharpies with male Cooper's Hawks is a common problem. Note tail shape, and the size of the head.

Immature streaked brown below with brown upperparts. In flight, note square corners at the tip of the tail, and how shoulders are hunched forward around the head.

Northern Goshawk

Accipiter gentilis

L 21–25" | **WS** 40–46"

Stealthy and fierce, the goshawk is a truculent broad-shouldered beast of a bird. A ghost of the northern woods, it is surprisingly elusive for such a large raptor, and ranks among our most sought-after birds. Common nowhere, some breed at scattered sites on the plateau in larger forest blocks especially along the northern edge of the state, especially where there are conifers. The goshawk is best seen by watching the skies at autumn hawk-watching sites such as Hawk Mountain Sanctuary, from mid-October to early December. In winter and early spring, goshawks are unpredictable in occurrence and can appear almost anywhere in the state, but generally are most at home away from civilization in remote, wild areas. An impressive hunter, it subsists on a diet of squirrels, grouse, crows, and other large birds. When not on the move, it roosts usually in dense wooded areas where it is hard to see.

Adult steely blue-gray above with white eyebrow, red eye, and gray underparts.

Juvenile has heavily streaked underparts; streaks usually extend to the undertail. Note graduated tail, and buff or pale checkering on the back.

Large size, big shoulders, pale eyebrow, and relatively broad tail. Puffy undertail coverts usually streaked on juveniles.

Red-shouldered Hawk

Buteo lineatus

L 20" | **WS** 40"

Though the Red-shouldered Hawk can be somewhat inconspicuous in winter, and especially near nesting sites, its raucous call
betrays its presence. The call is a far-carrying cry, a penetrating
KEE-yuh, KEE-yuh, KEE-yuh call that is alarming and
repeated at length. Regular along roadsides, but especially fond
of moist mixed or deciduous woodlands, and treed areas near
wetlands and along river valleys, the Red-shouldered is found
across the state throughout the year, though less commonly in
winter. Perching on branches in the mid-story of forests or just
below treetop level at forest edges, it looks out on water or open
areas, hoping to spy a frog, snake, or small rodent to snatch.
Look for it during migration in late March and early April, or at
autumn hawk-watching sites in October and November.

Adults reddish on breast
and shoulders with
checkered black-and-white
wings and banded tail.

Rough-legged Hawk
Buteo lagopus

L 18-20" | **WS** 52-54"

This attractive hawk, well-marked in black and white, is a
scarce migrant and winter visitor, occasionally seen here from
November into April. Well adapted to cold climates, almost
more feathers than flesh, it has a small bill and small feet,
feathered legs, and seems fluffy compared to other large hawks.
Breeding on the Arctic tundra, the Rough-legged Hawk favors
similar open habitats when here, including marshes and farm
fields. It may perch on posts or snags like other hawks, but
unlike others, when it perches atop a tree it usually chooses one
that is isolated and in the open, and sits amid the smaller outer
branches (other large hawks choose heavier branches). It preys
mostly upon rodents, hovering on long wings as it hunts, before
stooping into a dive or continuing to track an animal. As is
common in raptors, Rough-legged Hawks occur in two different
morphs. Dark morph individuals appear almost entirely
blackish, and light morphs (more prevalent in Pennsylvania)
are mostly white with black markings.

Pale morphs have
black belly patch, black
almost square-like
patches at bend of
wing, and pale head,
breast, and wings. Tail
is pale with dark
terminal band.

Dark morphs are
charcoal with paler
wings, and
pale-based tail
with dark band.

Red-tailed Hawk

Buteo jamaicensis

L 20" | **WS** 48.5"

A very large raptor, the chesty and broad Red-tailed Hawk is our most widely distributed and most regularly encountered hawk. Present year-round throughout the state, Red-taileds prey mostly on mammals such as meadow voles, squirrels, and rabbits. Even nesting in urban areas, they are most common along country roadsides and highways, or along the edges of forests and fields, where they often sound off regularly (especially when startled). The fierce, far-carrying cry is a shrill, screaming *SEE-uurrrrrr...*, explosive at the beginning, but trailing off at the end.

Large with mottled brown and white back; underparts white; conspicuous coppery red tail.

Mostly pale below but note streaky brown belly-band and brown band along leading edge of the underwing. Tail is less red below than above.

Juvenile is similar to adult but lacks red, instead showing a brown tail with black bars.

Virginia Rail

Rallus limicola

L 9" | **WS** 14"

Scurrying about marshes and wetland patches like a little
ruddy-shouldered orange-billed chicken, the Virginia Rail is far
more often heard than seen. Especially vocal in the spring, it
grunts a somewhat Three Stooges-like, grating *NYUK Nyuk-
nyuk-yuk-uk-uk-uk...* that is faster and quieter as it ends. It
also gives a ticking *kik kik kiddik kiddik kiddik*. Vocalizing in
the evening as often as in daylight, it migrates under the safety
of darkness. Rails are not maneuverable in flight and are
vulnerable to capture by hawks, so they are hesitant to fly in
daylight. They are secretive residents in reedy marshes and
rank wetland vegetation. The Virginia Rail is especially fond of
stands of cattails, and uses its slender body and strong legs to
slink around, hunting for insects, wetland invertebrates, and
small fish, seldom venturing out into view. Look (and listen!)
for it at marsh edges, or scooting across a trail before shooting
back into the marsh. Nesting at scattered spots across the state
(especially wetlands from Erie County south to Lawrence), it is
rarely detected in winter. Good spots to search include Heinz
NWR, marshes around Pymatuning, Geneva/Conneaut Marsh,
Julian Wetlands, Woods Edge Park, the Muck in Tioga County,
and wetlands of Susquehanna County.

Rarely out in the open as pictured;
note small size, gray cheeks, rufous
breast and shoulders, and
red-orange base of bill.

Sora

Porzana carolina

L 8.5" | **WS** 14"

A small, sneaky marsh bird, the Sora is much more often detected by its shrill vocalizations, than by sight. It gives both an upslurred *quee-EE, quee-EE* and a descending whinny, *KEEK, KI Ki ki ki ki* that trails off. A stealthy stalker of sedges and cattails, it often cocks its tail as it searches for prey, hunting the marsh and its edges for invertebrates and seeds. When alarmed it runs into vegetation, seldom taking flight except at night when migrating. It can turn up almost anywhere during migrations in April and May and in September and October. Absent in winter, it breeds at scattered sites around the state, with the largest numbers nesting in the extensive wetlands of the northwest, from Erie County south to Lawrence County.

Adult has yellow bill, black face with gray cheeks, and gray neck. Often walks with tail cocked up, revealing a white undertail.

Common Gallinule

Gallinula galeata

L 13" | **WS** 23"

Absent in winter, the gallinule is a dark wetland bird found in April through October at marshes or along the edges of ponds, lakes, and rivers with thick wetland vegetation. At times it walks amid reeds and cattails and can be quite secretive, but in other moments it walks on floating vegetation, using its long toes to steady it and spread its weight. It is also seen swimming duck-like in open water, pecking at the surface for seeds or other vegetable matter, and will up-end and even dive on occasion. It is an uncommon breeding bird, but some nest in wetlands of the northwest, with few nests elsewhere. When nesting, it can be vocal, including at night, and gives a laughing, descending, rapid whinny with a series or *hep* or *hrr* notes.

Adults have red bill and white along flanks, and a longish white patch along sides of the tail. Juveniles are dusky gray, with dark bill (lacking red/yellow), and paler throat.

American Coot

Fulica americana

L 16" **WS** 24"

Portly and dumpy, the American Coot seems to lack pretension, bobbing about on the water effortlessly or ambling around muddy or grassy areas with nary a care. It pecks at the water's surface and dives for food, and will also graze lawns. Despite a rather duck-like appearance, and with habits similar to ducks, the coot is actually in the rail family (with gallinule, Sora, Virginia Rail, and others). It even keeps company with ducks at ponds and lakes and is comfortable on open water, but also frequents marshy or swampy areas with emergent vegetation. In Pennsylvania it occurs mostly from September into May, and breeds here occasionally. Spring and fall are the best seasons to visit and seek it out at Harvey's Lake, Yellow Creek State Park, and other lakes or ponds with ducks or wetland birds.

Adult black overall with white bill, small dark knob on forehead, and small white patch on undertail. In flight note thin white trailing edge on wings. Juvenile paler gray overall, with darker grayish bill. When it walks on land, note its lobed toes.

Sandhill Crane

Grus canadensis

L 47" | **WS** 78.5"

Generally rare throughout the state, this stately five-foot-tall bird breeds in small numbers in the northwest in Lawrence, Mercer, and Crawford counties and toward the northeast in Bradford, Sullivan, and Columbia counties. It is rare in other areas, but in winter and during migration, cranes are spotted occasionally in farm fields, marshy grasslands, the edges of ponds, lakes or rivers, or as flyovers. Hawk-watching stations tally flying cranes every so often from September through November. Usually they are in small groups, but also occur singly, and some are first detected by voice as they utter pleasant, guttural bugling calls.

Strong wingbeats and steady fliers; fly with neck extended (not curled as with herons).

Very tall and silvery gray with long neck and legs. Adults have dark bill, and a red-brown cap. Juveniles lack red crown patch, and have more rust in plumage, especially on the wings.

Black-bellied Plover

Pluvialis squatarola

L 11" | **WS** 23"

This long-legged shorebird is our largest plover, and passes through as a migrant in spring and fall. An uncommon or local migrant, northbound Black-bellieds are seen in May, on their way to the Arctic breeding grounds. Southbound migrants move through from August to mid-October. It is rare on the plateau and in the mountains, and most sightings are from the southeast or near Lake Erie involving single birds or small flocks. Flyovers are seen occasionally, but more often it is observed running around in muddy areas, along beaches, shores of lakes or rivers, and in agricultural fields. The Black-bellied is vocal, giving a mellow *plee-oo-wee*, and it is wary and alert. It often calls in flight. Look for it at Presque Isle, Heinz NWR, Conejohela Flats, and other areas that attract shorebirds.

Distinctive breeding plumage is all black and white, with black belly and face, marbled white upperparts, and white crown.

Nonbreeding birds gray with grayish white crown. Note relatively heavy bill for a plover, and in flight look for the black "wingpits." Plovers have large eyes, compared to other shorebirds, as they are more visual hunters.

American Golden-Plover
Pluvialis dominica

L 9–11" | **WS** 22"

A classy shorebird, elegantly streamlined in shape, and built for long-distance migration from the Arctic to South America, this snazzy mid-size plover occurs here in migration. It's a hard bird to see here, occurring uncommonly or rarely from August through October, when most are juveniles or nonbreeding adults. They frequently keep company with Black-bellied Plovers on mudflats, farm fields, short grass at airports or turf farms. A conspicuous difference from Black-bellied is a smaller, more delicate bill. Spring migrants in breeding plumage are easy to identify with their gold-spangled upperparts and jet black underparts but are much rarer. Most sightings are from the southeast and the northwest.

Breeding adult black below all the way through the undertail, with distinct white stripe from eyebrow to shoulder. Look for gray "wingpits" in flight.

Juvenile similar to nonbreeding adult, but more spotted. Both show strong pale eyebrow and dark cap.

Semipalmated Plover

Charadrius semipalmatus

L 7" | **WS** 14"

Cute and round-headed, the Semipalmated is our smallest plover, seen scampering quickly along beaches or mudflats, and sometimes in farm fields. It runs in spurts, stopping periodically to nab an insect or pull at a worm, before continuing on. In agricultural areas it can be confused with (or mingle with) the larger Killdeer, but the Semipalmated has a single chest band and a shorter, stubbier bill. Like most shorebirds, it is found here only as a migrant, breeding far to our north in Canada and Alaska. It passes through fairly commonly as a migrant in May and from July through September. Often first detected by voice, it gives a high-pitched *cheh-wee* that rises on the second note.

Adult brown-backed, white below, with a single black band across the breast and yellow legs. In breeding season the bill is two-tone with a yellow-orange base but becomes darker and duskier in fall and winter.

Juvenile similar with brown back and chest band, but has pale scale-like fringes across the upperparts. Bill is dark and legs are dusky.

Killdeer

Charadrius vociferus

L 9" | **WS** 18.5"

One of few shorebirds nesting in Pennsylvania, this plover is among the most well-known birds in the state, famous for gracing farm fields and open country statewide throughout the year. The Killdeer is named for its loud piercing call, given most often in flight as *kill-dee, kill-dee,* and often repeated. Well known for placing its nest, which is little more than a scrape in the ground, in the middle of gravel roads, the Killdeer will make a racket as people approach the nest. In such situations it also performs a distraction display in which it feigns a broken wing, dragging one wing while running from the nest, in an attempt to steer trouble away from the eggs or young. It feeds similarly to other plovers, running in spurts and stopping to grab at prey on the ground.

Large plover with two black bands across the breast. Long tail is mostly brick-red with black band.

Greater Yellowlegs

Tringa melanoleuca

L 13.5" | **WS** 27.5"

Lanky and tall, this shorebird is an active wader inhabiting a variety of wetland habitats, striding about at the edges of large ponds, lakes, rivers, wet meadows, and working shallows around marshes or mudflats. As it walks, it sweeps its bill back and forth, stirring the water for invertebrates and other prey. Sometimes it runs for short bursts and can wade amid deeper waters than other shorebirds, but often keeps company with dowitchers and especially Lesser Yellowlegs. It is similar in habits and appearance to the more numerous Lesser Yellowlegs, but the two differ in size, shape, and sounds. Absent in winter and nesting in Canada and Alaska, the Greater Yellowlegs is a fairly widespread migrant in April and May and again from July to November. Often it is heard before it is seen, giving a shrill, strident *tyew! tyew! tyew!* that is heard even at some distance. Good spots to check for it include Pymatuning, Yellow Creek State Park, Conejohela Flats, and Heinz NWR.

Large, with long yellow legs, and long neck. Long bill is slightly upcurved and nearly twice the length of the head.

Lesser Yellowlegs

Tringa flavipes

L 10" | **WS** 27"

A smaller, scaled-down version of the Greater Yellowlegs, the Lesser is the more numerous migrant in Pennsylvania. Breeding to our north in the subarctic taiga, it winters along the coast from Virginia south, heading north through here in April and May and then returning July through October. It is a fairly common migrant across the state, visiting mudflats, marshy pools, ponds, wet meadows, and grassy margins of lakes and rivers. Similar in habits to the Greater, the Lesser Yellowlegs wades in shallow water, sometimes trotting after prey, or engaging other shorebirds in little skirmishes at feeding areas. Large groups may gather at Heinz NWR and Conejohela Flats, and look for them around Pymatuning Lake and Lake Somerset. Listen for the *tew tew* call; not as loud or shrill as the more vocal Greater Yellowlegs.

Darker overall, and smaller with a thinner, shorter bill compared to Greater Yellowlegs. Usually the bill is only a little longer than the head. Lesser also has less pale gray at the base of the bill.

Spotted Sandpiper
Actitis macularius

L 7.5" | **WS** 15"

The jaunty Spotted Sandpiper is a welcome sight, teetering along streams and wetland edges across the state. Found around ponds, lakes, rivers, and man-made water bodies, unlike most other shorebirds it also works rocky or stony shorelines with gravel. Moving with quick steps, when it pauses it habitually bobs up and down before striding on in search of insects or other prey. When excited, it takes to the air, giving a rapid ringing *pweet pweet pweet* call, and flying with a unique stutter-flutter in which bouts of rapid pulsing wingbeats are interrupted by glides with the wings angled down. It is absent in winter, but common here from April into October, and the eponymous spots are present only on breeding adults in the spring and early summer. One of just five species of shorebirds nesting in Pennsylvania, it breeds widely across the state but is a generally uncommon breeding bird.

Breeding adults are spotted below. Brown upperparts are barred with blackish. Nonbreeders lack spots, but are white below and show a brown smudge at sides of breast.

Juveniles are white below with buffy barring above, especially at shoulder. In flight, a white stripe in wing is visible (present at all ages).

Solitary Sandpiper
Tringa solitaria

L 7-9" | **WS** 16"

As its name suggests, the Solitary Sandpiper is often seen singly, preferring secluded ponds, ditches or puddles with grass, or treed swampy areas. It is less often on open mudflats or in open water but usually tucked away in the corner of a grassy pool, jerking its head up and down as it eyes up the scene. Often it is not seen until it flushes when approached, usually before you even know it is there. When flying, it shows dark blackish underwings, and lets loose with a shrill, piping "see Pete!" or "see see Pete" call. It calls at night, too, while migrating. Wintering in South America and breeding in boreal forests of Canada and Alaska, Solitary Sandpiper passes through Pennsylvania as a widespread yet uncommon migrant in April and May and again from July to October. As shorebirds go, the Solitary has a medium-length bill and moderately long legs.

Mostly dark above with grayish brown head and white eye ring, clean white belly and greenish legs. Dark underwings in flight are different from yellowlegs or Spotted Sandpiper.

Upland Sandpiper

Bartramia longicauda

L 11-12 | **"WS** 18-22"

When seen amid its preferred dry grassland habitat, with its long tail, small head and doe eyes, this odd shorebird hardly recalls a sandpiper. In fact, being large and beautifully marbled in straw-brown, this bird is most closely related to curlews. It runs in furrows of plowed fields, or walks in open grassy areas such as airstrips, golf courses, or turf farms, behaving more like a grassland plover than a sandpiper. Famous as a long-distance migrant and wintering in South America, they breed in grasslands in Canada and the U.S., but only a few pairs nest in Pennsylvania, mostly in the western half and primarily in grassy reclaimed strip mines. Seen here between May and September, they are not easy to find as migrants, but search for them in grassy fields, especially in southern Clarion County, the Pymatuning area, or along Sandy Ridge Road in Clearfield County, where they breed. Uplands have the remarkable habit of sitting atop posts, and every so often launch themselves into aerial display in which they belt out a dramatic drawn-out whistle. More often they give a throaty rattle, and are active even at night.

A brown "grasspiper" with straight yellowish bill with black tip. Note yellow legs and white belly.

Pectoral Sandpiper

Calidris melanotos

L 8.5" | **WS** 17"

A chunky shorebird, the Pectoral Sandpiper is named for its contrasting chest pattern in which the streaky brown throat and chest are sharply demarcated from the white belly. Migrating impressive distances from its Arctic breeding grounds to South America, the Pectoral passes through Pennsylvania heading northbound in April and May, and moving south from July into October. Mostly avoiding the plateau, it occurs fairly widely otherwise, and is seen working wet grassy areas, mudflats, muddy fields, and shorelines for invertebrates, and it vocalizes frequently. Calling most often when in flight, the common call is a harsh, grating *churt*. Good spots to check for Pectorals include Heinz NWR, Yellow Creek State Park, and around Pymatuning Lake and Shenango Reservoir.

Medium-size, with moderate, slightly droopy bill, and yellowish legs. Heavily marked breast contrasts sharply with white belly. Juveniles less crisply patterned.

Ruddy Turnstone
Arenaria interpres

L 7" | **WS** 21"

Breeding in the Arctic, this dapper shorebird is known in places as the "calico-back" for its contrasting plumage. Widely known for its habit of overturning stones with its straight and pointed bill while searching for food, the turnstone winters on tropical beaches and stony shorelines throughout the world. In Pennsylvania it is a scarce or rare visitor, seen on occasion along the Lake Erie shoreline and rarely elsewhere. Look for this stocky, short-legged shorebird at Presque Isle where it shows up sometimes in small numbers in May and June or in August and September. It is also seen once in a while along the Susquehanna River, especially at the Conejohela Flats, either singly or in small groups. In flight it shows a striking black-and-white wing pattern, and often calls giving a rapid rattled *tu tu tu tu* or *ki ki ki* call.

In breeding plumage shows calico markings with rust color on the back and curvy black lines on head and neck.

Nonbreeding birds are darker, with darker head and browner back. In flight note white on the back, the base of the tail, and the wing stripe.

Sanderling
Calidris alba

L 7.5" | **WS** 13.5"

Well known for running along with the ebb and flow of the ocean's edge, Sanderlings are found at beaches across the globe. They nest in the high Arctic, and are generally rare in Pennsylvania, regular only at Lake Erie and less often along the lower Susquehanna River. Most sightings here are of southbound migrants in August and September, either at Presque Isle or at the Conejohela Flats, but occasionally they show up in May. They prefer sandy beaches but also use mudflats or muddy shorelines. They often seem plump when at rest, but foraging birds speed by quickly, feeding between bouts of running. Frequently they are in small groups and like other migrating birds, inclement weather may push Sanderlings out of the sky and down onto the best available habitat. Keep an eye out for them, and other shorebirds, after storms in summer or fall.

Reddish in breeding plumage (especially males), the Sanderling is a small sandpiper with a medium-short, straight bill.

Nonbreeding adults are mostly white with a dark shoulder patch. Juveniles are similar but are more checkered black and white on the back.

Stilt Sandpiper

Calidris himantopus

L 8.5" | **WS** 16.5"

Medium-size and relatively tall with a medium-length slightly downcurved bill, the Stilt Sandpiper is relatively quiet and overlooked amid other shorebirds. With its long legs, it wades in open pools, often with yellowlegs or dowitchers, but also uses mudflats and beaches for feeding. Though they migrate north through the middle of the continent to Arctic breeding grounds, almost all sightings in Pennsylvania are from August to early October when they are headed south, and only rarely is one seen in May. Their occurrence in the state varies by the year, but they are generally uncommon to rare. The lanky Stilt Sandpiper is best sought on the shore of Lake Erie or along the lower Susquehanna River. Not particularly vocal for a shorebird and with a quiet call, it is less often heard than the birds it consorts with, but occasionally offers scratchy squeaks, or a sharp *pieu!*

Pale gray with long greenish yellow legs; note how the black longish bill droops slightly. Pale eyebrows set off by darker cap.

Dunlin
Calidris alpina

L 7" | **WS** 14.5"

The plump Dunlin is perhaps the prototypical sandpiper. This small shorebird is fairly common in spring migration in April and May and is seen heading south in October and November. A hardy sandpiper, Dunlins continue to migrate later in the fall, after almost all other shorebirds have finished passing through. Foraging on mudflats at the edges of marshes, lakes, and rivers, and roosting and feeding on beaches or in flooded fields, the Dunlin is a common migrant at Lake Erie and at other wetlands in the northwest, and is also regular at a variety of locations in the southeast. Look for it at Presque Isle, Pymatuning, Yellow Creek State Park, and at shorebird spots along the Susquehanna and Delaware rivers.

In spring and summer, adults are reddish above with black on belly.

Medium-size with long, drooping bill and black legs; relatively dark gray-brown above, with brownish bib.

White-rumped Sandpiper
Calidris fuscicollis

L 6.5" | **WS** 16.5"

A sandpiper with long, pointed wings, the White-rumped Sandpiper is a long-distance migrant, passing through in small numbers in May and in August and September. Nesting in the Arctic and wintering in South America, it occasionally shows up on beaches, mudflats, at the edges of ponds, lakes, and rivers. Most are seen in the northwest and southeast of the state, and good places to check include the Conejohela Flats, and Heinz NWR, but look for them to be grounded in wetlands after storms. Often the White-rumped mingles with other small sandpipers (collectively often referred to as "peep"), such as Least or Semi-palmated Sandpipers, and it is slightly larger and longer-winged than these. The namesake white rump can be tough to see, but is best seen when the bird is flying directly away from an observer.

Small, with very long wings that extend beyond the tail tip. Streaky chest with faint streaks or chevrons down the flanks. Tiny orangish patch at base of bill. In flight, look for the entirely white rump.

Baird's Sandpiper

Calidris bairdii

L 5-7" | **WS** 13-15"

The slender Baird's Sandpiper is a scarce migrant in Pennsylvania. Breeding in the Arctic and wintering in South America, nearly all seen here are sandy brown juveniles in August and September. Occasionally one is seen wading in shallow water, but compared to most other sandpipers it is usually in drier areas, preferring sandy beaches and mudflats. It makes use of areas with a very short crop of grass, including shorelines and turf farms.

Long wings that extend past the tail make a pointed rear end. Juvenile's back is beautifully scaled and scalloped with black-centered feathers fringed white. Warm sandy brown above, with buff or brown bib, and white belly. Bill is thin and moderately long.

Semipalmated Sandpiper

Calidris pusilla

L 6" | **WS** 12"

The stubby little Semipalmated Sandpiper seems rather nondescript, but its combination of its shape, small size, and black bill and legs set it apart from the others. This pale gray "peep" (small sandpiper) is fussy and vocal, and it giggles a rapid *wee-dee-dee-dee-dee* as it runs around on the mud. It is often seen in the same general area that Least Sandpipers forage, but the Semi prefers to be out in wet muddy spots. It is sometimes in good-size flocks, and it sometimes engages aggressively with other pipers nearby, cocking up its tail and chattering away at those feeding too closely. It is named for its partially webbed toes, a feature that is hard to see, but one that sets it apart from most of its relatives. Breeding in the Arctic, its migration takes it through Pennsylvania in May and southward in late July through October. It is fairly common along the shore of Lake Erie, in the southeast (check Heinz NWR and Conejohela Flats), and regular if less common along the rivers in the southwest. Fall migrants are most numerous during drought years.

Small with a straight, peg-like, blunt bill, and black legs. Adults are grayish above with black spots on back.

Least Sandpiper

Calidris minutilla

L 5.5-6" | **WS** 11"

The world's smallest shorebird is also our state's most widely encountered sandpiper. Weighing only as much as a bit of pocket change, this charming brown "peep" is a common migrant nearly throughout the state. They move north through here in May, return in July, and continue to move south into October. Sometimes they are in small flocks, found along beaches and in muddy areas. They often prefer flats with very short grass, and crouch down more often than other small sandpipers. The Least is a vocal shorebird, especially in flight. When a Least Sandpiper takes to the air, it almost says its name, emitting a mousy *least!*

Darker and browner than other "peeps"; note tiny size, and short bill that droops slightly at the tip. Bill tip is thinner than Semipalmated. Legs are yellowish.

Juveniles are warm brown above with reddish highlights and fine white spots on back. Smaller than Semipalmated.

Short-billed Dowitcher

Limnodromus griseus

L 11" | **WS** 19"

Short-billed Dowitchers forage in shallow open water or mud, using a distinctive, rapid, up and down sewing-machine-like motion. Often these dowitchers keep company with yellowlegs in marshy ponds, pools, mudflats, and along shorelines, and when they take flight they reveal a white back patch and vocalize. The Short-billed Dowitcher's call is less shrill than those of many shorebirds, as it mutters its chirpy *tu-tu-tu or chitoo-too-too*. Breeding in the Arctic, they migrate through in May, especially at Presque Isle, then head back south from July to September. They are fairly common to uncommon in the southeast and the north-west, less common in the southwest, and occasionally are found in wetlands around State College. The Short-billed Dowitcher is extremely similar to the Long-billed Dowitcher (*Limnodromus scolopaceus*), which is only a rare visitor. The two differ most dramatically in vocalizations, with Long-billed giving a high-pitched *keeq* or *kweep*. Listen for sounds as they take flight.

Medium-size, fairly dark overall. Brownish adults show significant reddish on neck. Note long, straight bill. Feeds with sewing-machine-like action, probing straight up and down in mud or water.

In flight, note the long bill and white stripe up the back.

The Long-billed Dowitcher (*Limnodromus scolopaceus*) has a very long bill that usually seems kinked slightly downward toward the tip. Juveniles show plain brown-gray tertials with thin red fringes (in juvenile Short-billed, these feathers have wavy bars).

Wilson's Snipe

Gallinago delicata

L 11.5" | **WS** 17"

Cryptically patterned in beautiful buff, brown, and black, the sneaky snipe is good at remaining out of sight amid mucky marshes, moist meadows and pastures, small grassy puddles, flooded fields, roadside ditches, and other boggy habitats. When approached, the snipe remains motionless as long as possible before exploding into the air in rapid, irregular, zig-zag movements, often calling out as it goes. Giving a hushed *snape* sound, it may settle in again only a short distance away, but vanish amid the bumpy, muddy terrain it prefers. A scarce breeder in Pennsylvania, especially in Warren, McKean, Somerset, and Bedford counties, the snipe is most often encountered when migrating in March and April or when southbound in October and November. Migrants are occasionally found in winter. Look for it at Yellow Creek State Park, Imperial Grasslands, and at wetlands along the Susquehanna and Delaware rivers.

Secretive and wary. Note long, straight bill, and straw-buff back stripes offset by black and brown feathering. White below with short legs.

American Woodcock

Scolopax minor

L 11" | **WS** 18"

Odd and endearing, this unique retiring shorebird prefers damp woodlands and meadows. Its peculiar nature has led to the bestowal of a variety of colloquial names, including "timber-doodle" and "Labrador twister." Largely nocturnal, the woodcock hunts worms in moist, open ground, and if seen during the day it is usually only when accidentally flushed from the forest floor or from patches of shrubs and dogwoods. In flight the woodcock buzzes away quickly with audible whistling wingbeats, and moves somewhat like a flying saucer, but exhibiting odd proportions. Though present throughout the year, it is most conspicuous in late winter and spring, when the sharp insect-like call, commonly transliterated as *peeent!* is heard at dusk. On the breeding grounds, it engages in spectacular aerial displays, fluttering around up high with chittering calls, before making a rapid descent to the ground.

Note odd eye position, which allows it to see behind its head. Rotund body, with buffy underparts, and long bill.

Bonaparte's Gull

Chroicocephalus philadelphia

L 13" | **WS** 30.5"

A petite, dainty gull, the Bonaparte's Gull occurs in Pennsylvania as a migrant and winter visitor. It is most often seen on the northbound migration in March and April, but is also seen in fall in November and December. Found on lakes and rivers and sometimes in wet agricultural fields, nearly any decent-size body of water can host this species. Thousands are sometimes found on Lake Erie, and many migrate north in spring along the Susquehanna. Check water bodies during migration months after storms, as severe weather can ground migrating flocks. This small gull is named for Napoleon's nephew, Charles Lucien Bonaparte, who lived in New Jersey and Philadelphia in the 1820s and described many new American bird species.

Small with delicate proportions, fine bill, and a white leading edge to the pointed, tapering wings. Buoyant and tern-like in flight, but note squared off tail. Breeding adults have black head.

Winter adults have white head with black ear spot. Immature has dark outline to wings and a black tail band.

Laughing Gull
Leucophaeus atricilla

L 16" | **WS** 40"

Throwing its head back and craning its neck, the slender Laughing Gull lets loose with a raucous laughing cry. A social, conspicuous gull, its sounds are emblematic of summer along the mid-Atlantic coast of the U.S., and it is a handsome bird. Mostly it hangs close to the ocean, but it also occurs inland along waterways into southeastern Pennsylvania. Very common on the coastal plain from April into October, it rests in parking lots and parks along rivers, especially along the lower Delaware River and uncommonly to the lower Susquehanna. It is scarce or rare elsewhere in the state, but storms sometimes drive numbers of Laughing Gulls inland. Look for it at the Delaware River Trail in Philadelphia, and at Pennypack on the Delaware.

Breeding adults have black head, slate gray back, and solid black wing tips. The bill is reddish at the peak of breeding plumage but gradually turns black after the breeding season. By autumn the head becomes pale dusky with a smudgy black ear patch.

Juvenile is brown with a white rump. Note slender shape and very pointed wings in flight.

Ring-billed Gull

Larus delawarensis

L 19" | **WS** 43.5"

A medium-size gull, the Ring-billed Gull is commonly encountered throughout most of the state. Making itself at home in mall parking lots, around fast food joints, and at water bodies, this is the typical "seagull" that even casual observers note during their day-to-day routines when shopping and running errands. Its numbers swell in winter, and sometimes large flocks gather at lakes, rivers, fields, and landfills. Their numbers thin out a bit in summer but are still regular in the southeast and northwest. Some have nested in Erie County.

Adults have a yellow bill with an obvious black ring. The head becomes streaky in winter, but is bright white in summer.

First-year Ring-billed has a two-tone bill pink at base with black tip, pinkish legs, and pale gray back, with contrasting brownish feathers at the shoulder. In flight the tail is mostly white with dark band at the tip.

Herring Gull
Larus argentatus

L 24" | **WS** 55.5"

Mostly absent from the central and northern plateau regions, the
hefty Herring Gull is otherwise fairly widespread and common on
lakes, large rivers, and at landfills. It breeds mostly north of our
state, but some Herring Gulls nest around Pittsburgh along the
Ohio and Allegheny rivers. Generally their numbers in Pennsylvania dip in summer and rise in winter. Large flocks aggregate in
winter at Lake Erie, around Pittsburgh, and in the southeast.
Counts of over 100,000 have been tallied in winter at landfills in
Bucks County. After three or four years, a Herring Gull shows the
familiar adult plumage; it is born brown overall with a mostly
dark bill, and then undergoes gradual cycles of feather replace-
ment. Second-year birds are intermediate in appearance.

Large gull with big head, long
heavy bill, an evenly gray
back, and pinkish legs.

First-year is variable but
brownish overall. Note
the large size, blocky
head, and heavy bill.

Lesser Black-backed Gull

Larus fuscus

L 21" | **WS** 54"

The Lesser Black-backed Gull is increasingly reported by birders in Pennsylvania. Mostly seen from October through April, it is generally uncommon in the southeast, but is locally common in Bucks County and along the Delaware and Susquehanna rivers. Elsewhere it is uncommon or rare, but is annual at Lake Erie and increasing in the Pittsburgh area in winter. Typically it is found around lakes, rivers or landfills. Often the Lesser Black-backed keeps company with Herring Gulls, and is conspicuous by virtue of its darker back, smaller size, and yellow legs. Like other gulls, it takes a couple of years to reach adult plumage.

Fairly large, slender, with noticeably long, pointed wings, and a shortish bill. Adults have slate-gray back and yellow legs. The head is streaky in winter.

Great Black-backed Gull

Larus marinus

L 30" | **WS** 65"

A brute of a gull, this is the largest gull species in the world. Heavy and powerful, it is a fearless and intimidating bird of our large lakes and rivers. Usually seen loafing at marinas and boatyards, roosting on sandbars and islands, or patrolling shorelines, it is a bully, chasing other gulls to steal food, and even killing birds such as coots or grebes. Its numbers thin out in summer and swell in winter. It is common along the Delaware and Susquehanna rivers, but is less common elsewhere in the southeast. It is also common at Lake Erie, but is mostly absent from the western and northern parts of the state.

Very large, broad, and fierce with big blocky head, heavy bill, and thick neck. Adult has black back, yellow bill, and chalky pinkish legs.

Juvenile is checkered above, streaky gray below with whitish head, and heavy black bill.

Caspian Tern

Hydroprogne caspia

L 20" | **WS** 50"

This gull-size tern is the largest tern species in the world. It cruises around lakes, rivers, and marshes with open water, and is quite vocal, calling often in flight. Like other large terns, the calls of adults and juveniles differ: adult Caspians give a loud harsh, rasping *ree-alp;* juveniles give a high-pitched whistled *ree-peeu.* Seen mostly in the southeast and northwest of the state, it occurs both in spring migration in April and May, and when returning south from July into September. Look for it along the lower Delaware River at Little Tinicum Island and at Heinz NWR, at Presque Isle, along the Susquehanna, and at Yellow Creek State Park.

Larger than some gulls, with heavy, red-orange bill, and neat black cap. Cap is streakier, less black, in winter and on juveniles.

Note heavy build and large head, and in flight see the broad wings, short tail, and extensive black on the underside of the wing tips. Bill is often pointed downward as it flies.

Black Tern

Chlidonias niger

L 9.5" | **WS** 23"

Dainty and dashing, nesting in freshwater marshes in southern Canada and the upper edge of the Lower 48, the Black Tern occurs here as an uncommon or rare migrant. Though it breeds on occasion in Crawford and Erie counties, mostly we see this attractive shadowy tern as a migrant in May or in August and September. It migrates along rivers and is seen flying over lakes, impoundments and large ponds, floating buoyantly and gracefully on the wing. With deep wingbeats, it swoops and jabs, grabbing insects and other food from the water's surface. Search for it in wetlands of the northwest including marshes around Pymatuning, at Yellow Creek State Park, and along the Susquehanna and Delaware rivers.

A small marsh tern, its combination of a black body, slate gray wings, and white undertail is distinctive.

Nonbreeding birds are blackish gray above with black cap, black ear spot, and dusky black collar extending onto breast sides. White underneath like other terns, but note style of flight and short squared-off tail.

Common Tern
Sterna hirundo

L 12-15" | **WS** 30.5"

Slender and long-tailed, the Common Tern is uncommon or rare in most of the state but is regular at Presque Isle and is occasionally seen also along the Susquehanna and Delaware rivers. Wintering in South America, migrants are seen here from April to October, flying along rivers, or lakes, or roosting among groups of Forster's Terns on sandbars, mudflats, or other places that terns gather. When foraging, it flies usually only a few meters over the water, diving suddenly when it spots a fish, plunging into the water, and beating its way back into flight. The Common Tern is similar in appearance to the more widespread Forster's Tern, but is more slender, and gray-bodied, with a darker gray back. Nonbreeding adults and juvenile Commons have a mostly black rear crown, and a blackish bar along the shoulder. The call is an abrupt high *kik, kik* or a longer drawn out *klee-yehhh.*

Breeding adult has black cap, and is pale overall but with gray body, rump and wings. White tail contrasts with gray back, and white undertail contrasts with gray belly.

Forster's Tern

Sterna forsteri

L 13.5" | **WS** 31"

The Forster's is a beautiful tern with long, pointed wings and a long, forked white tail. It is elegant in appearance and in its movements, flying with grace but dogged and determined when feeding, making quick darting dives for fish. It is found around lakes, rivers, and marshy areas with open water. When a Forster's hits the water, it quickly takes off again, shaking itself off and giving hoarse, reedy *herr* calls, or making more excited, abrupt *kip, kip* sounds. Common from April to August at Lake Erie and along the Delaware and Susquehanna rivers, it is less common elsewhere, but is still the most regularly encountered tern away from these areas. Storms sometimes push them around, scattering them at sites where they are otherwise uncommon or rare, and migrants can turn up in surprising places.

Breeding adults are clean pearly grayish white above, with bright white outer wing, black cap, and orange-yellow bill with black tip.

Nonbreeding birds have black eye patch and white crown.

Rock Pigeon

Columba livia

L 13" | **WS** 23"

Familiar to all, some among us find real charm in the rotund Rock Pigeon as it waddles along, cooing away. Large groups of pigeons gather in city parks where residents enjoying feeding them, and in such situations, males are often observed displaying to females, puffing themselves up and walking after the female, making a variety of pleasant low-pitched hoots and coos. When they take flight, one can hear the wings whistle, or smack together as the wings meet over the back. While easy to identify when waddling along in a park, the pigeon is a shape-shifter in the air, taking on a deceptive array of appearances. A dynamic flyer, it can look like a falcon when moving rapidly, and pigeon flocks can also look quite like shorebirds or ducks at times. Widespread domestication has yielded a range of plumage variations, with rust, slate-gray, and white varieties, among others. This bird is not native to America, but was introduced from Eurasia where it evolved as a cliff-dwelling bird, so its use of bridges and urban landscapes with tall buildings makes sense. But the pigeon is also at home in suburban areas and farm country.

Typically pale gray, with darker gray head, and some greenish on the neck. In flight note white rump and underwings, and dark tail band.

Mourning Dove

Zenaida macroura

L 11" | **WS** 17.5"

With its skinny neck and small head, the Mourning Dove is shaped unlike any other common bird in the state. Perching on utility wires along roads, and in a great variety of habitats year-round, this is one of the most widespread and abundant birds in the countryside. Sometimes they are in small groups of a handful or more, feeding on seeds on the ground. When startled, they take to the air, their wings whistle, and they reveal a distinctive black and white tail pattern. Their flight is strong, fast and direct with quick, shallow wing beats, and they can change direction abruptly. Its somber call is frequently mistaken for an owl, and is often given near dusk. The typical call is a *who WHO, whoo whoo whoo...* sometimes repeated for many minutes.

Tan and slender with a long, pointed tail. Black spot on ear and spots on wings. White in outer tail visible when taking flight.

Yellow-billed Cuckoo

Coccyzus americanus

L 12" | **WS** 16"

A sleuth of woodlands, thickets and brushy hedgerows from May to September, this stealthy bird is known in places as the "rain crow" for its habit of calling out on steamy days in advance of storms, in response to the distant rumble of thunder. It is indeed a vocal bird, giving several distinctive calls including a *kik kik kik keh-OW, keh-OW, k-OW, kow, kow* or a more plaintive *tu-oh tu-oh tu-oh*. Typically solitary, it moves surreptitiously in cover, as it searches for its favored food, tent caterpillars. When perched it turns slowly like a reptile, and may sit tucked away amid the foliage for minutes on end. Though widespread in spring and summer, often it is seen just fleetingly as it flies across a road or a trail before vanishing again into the foliage. In the air it reveals a long tail, white underparts, and rufous wings.

Slender with long tail, and white below, with large white tail spots. Bill is mostly yellow, and yellow eye ring.

Black-billed Cuckoo

Coccyzus erythropthalmus

L 12" | **WS** 16"

The Black-billed Cuckoo nests in large tracts of forest across most of the state. Though fairly widespread as a breeder and a migrant from May through September, it is heard far more often than it is seen. Despite its persistent hollow-sounding *koo koo koo koo*, it can be very frustrating trying to see this bird as it calls away while hidden deep in cover. Feeding on caterpillars and moth larvae, it likes to stay inside of thick foliage and dense forest, but migrants are sometimes seen in more open areas. In general, its habits are similar to the Yellow-billed Cuckoo, and both pass winter in South America, but Black-billed seems to prefer slightly thicker, shadier vegetation.

Very slender, with dark bill and grayish spots on underside of tail. Little or no rufous in wings. Throat is grayish or creamy buff, compared to the heavier Yellow-billed's whiter throat. Adults have red eye ring. Juveniles have buffier throat and yellowish eye ring.

Barn Owl

Tyto alba

L 14" | **WS** 44"

Entirely nocturnal and comfortable hunting even in complete darkness, the lanky and round-faced Barn Owl is a ghost of the night. Frequenting farms surrounded by grasslands in the mountains and Piedmont, it hunts for mice using its acute sense of hearing, which is aided by its round facial discs that direct sound to its ears. During the day it roosts, hidden in dense stands of trees, atop silos, or in dark corners of barns and abandoned buildings. Given its habits and a population in decline due to changes in land use, it is not an easy bird to see. But its voice often betrays a Barn Owl's presence, and at night the alarming call is a chilling, raspy screech—a sound befitting a particularly frightening moment in a horror film. It is, however, the "friend of the farmer" and consumes large numbers of small rodents. The owls nest in cavities including farm buildings and can be attracted to nest boxes.

Mostly white in the face and belly, it is buff and gray on the back. Female buffier than male, with more spotting on chest. Note long legs and dark eyes.

Snowy Owl
Bubo scandiacus

L 20-28" | **WS** 50-57"

Large, powerful and white overall, surely the Snowy Owl is among the most sought-after and charismatic birds in the world. This Arctic owl is almost as much a myth in people's minds as it is a part of the state's wildlife, but it is highly nomadic and only a semi-regular visitor to Pennsylvania. Rare and unpredictable from December to March, in many years only a few are seen in the state, but during invasion years (perhaps once every 8 or 10 years) dozens may grace the commonwealth. A bird of the tundra, when here the Snowy Owl also prefers expanses of open ground, frequenting airports, farm fields, and shorelines. Occasionally one even surprises people by perching on a building or a post in a town or a city. Mostly solitary, they are active both at night and during the day, hunting rodents and ducks, and scavenging at carcasses at times too.

Rare. Very large with yellow eyes. Plumage is variable: some almost entirely white, others heavily marked with brown or black barring and spots.

Eastern Screech-Owl

Megascops asio

L 8.5" | **WS** 20"

A cute reddish or gray owl, the Eastern Screech-Owl is widespread and occurs here commonly year-round. At home in small or medium-size woodlots in rural and suburban areas, it is less common in urban areas and large expanses of forest. Active only at night, its descending whinny call and its monotone trill are among our most commonly heard nocturnal bird sounds. Occasionally it will vocalize from its roost during the day, but the screech-owl is usually inconspicuous when the sun is out and hard to see, and even when vocalizing it is hard to spot. A master of camouflage, beautifully marbled, two different color morphs occur here. Rufous or red morph screech-owls often roost amid brownish dead leaves, blending in remarkably, while gray morphs blend spectacularly into the neighboring bark and branches. At times though, the screech-owl fails to realize it is roosting in plain sight, and alert observers may spot one sitting motionless and sleepy in a nest box or in a hole in tree in the backyard.

Small size, yellow eyes, crosshatched breast pattern, and black stripes frame the face. Gray morph is more common in Pennsylvania, and shows black streaks and white spotting.

Red morph is distinctive, as this is the only small rufous owl. Patterned the same as gray morph. Yellow eyes are often shut during the day, and ear tufts vary depending on the bird's mood.

Northern Saw-whet Owl

Aegolius acadicus

L 7.5" | **WS** 17.5"

Impossibly charismatic, this tiny owl is among our most sought-after birds, and its appeal is so undeniable that its likeness graces many of the state's conservation license plates. It is unthinkable that a person should not be captivated by the Saw-whet Owl. It has been the focus of much recent research in Pennsylvania, and is now known to be a fairly common migrant nearly statewide and a regular breeder, though its retiring habits mean that it is seldom seen. Active only at night when hunting mice and large insects, it occupies a variety of habitats, including swampy woodlands, thick stands of evergreens, brushy thickets, and mixed woodlands. It nests mostly in larger forests with a shrubby understory. Roosting amid dense vegetation, inside dense tangles of honeysuckle, or in thickly canopied conifers, it is hard to spot during the day. Most sightings occur between November and March, and migration peaks in April and then from October to December. During the breeding season, good numbers nest in McKean and Elk counties, and between Clearfield and Lackawanna counties especially at North Mountain. It also nests sparsely elsewhere in the mountains.

Tiny and cute, with big yellow eyes (sometimes shut during the day). Round brownish head is finely streaked with white. Blurry brown streaking below.

Great Horned Owl

Bubo virginianus

L 21.5" | **WS** 48.5"

Imposing and fierce, the unamused, "all-business" gaze of the Great Horned Owl is profound and noble. An adaptable year-round resident, it is seen in woodlots and fragmented forest, and is fond of edge habitats, occasionally perching at the edge of woodlands to take in the gathering dusk or watch the sun as it nears the horizon. It is heard calling on many evenings throughout the year. Males and females pair up in January and are heard duetting just before and after sunset, with the male's *whoo huh-ha whoo whoo* being deeper and more resonant than the female's call, which is otherwise similar in cadence. Taking rats, voles, rabbits, and other mammals during the darkness, the Great Horned Owl is a fearless predator and drives away or kills other owl species near its territory. Like other owls, it swallows its prey whole, later regurgitating pellets of indigestible fur and bones. These accumulate below roosting sites, with "whitewash" (excrement), and offer clues as to how and where an owl is spending its time.

Very large, broad-shouldered, wide-faced, with rounded chestnut-brown facial discs. Variable white throat patch is bordered with black below.

Barred Owl

Strix varia

L 20" | **WS** 42"

Locking eyes with the dark-eyed soulful stare of a Barred Owl is a thrilling moment. This bird is a spirit of dense woodlands, swampy forests, and other large expanses of trees in the north of the state and the high plateau. Present year-round here, it is fairly widespread across the state, but is generally uncommon. Look for it at Allegheny National Forest and in forests in Centre and Huntington counties, on North Mountain, and listen for its spectacular call. A superb vocalist, the typical call is often described as "Who cooks for you, who cooks for yooou all." Its sounds are loud, and it also gives a laughing, hooting *ha ha ha ha-how,* and some rolling, quavering howls. Calling sometimes even in daylight, it is generally more active during the day compared to other owls, and is seen roosting conspicuously on heavy branches within the forest or at the woods' edge.

Large, dark-eyed, gray with a pale bill. Dark eyebrows frame pale face, and note vertical streaks on belly. Round-headed, and lacks ear tufts.

Long-eared Owl

Asio otus

L 14.5" | **WS** 35–39"

Among our most handsome and elusive night birds, the Long-eared Owl is marked beautifully with rich brown and gray tones, and intricate crosshatched marbling and spotting. True to its name, the black ear tufts are long, usually projecting noticeably upward from the crown. Roosting during the day in stands of evergreens or mixed woodlots near open areas for hunting mice, its retiring nature, and nocturnal habits dictate that sightings of this elegant owl are few and far between. Generally it is scarce across the state, but probably it resides in parts of the state year-round, and migrants are seen in places such as Presque Isle SP. Its secretive habits obscure its exact status, but migration is in April and November, and many sightings are in winter between December and February. Nests are even discovered on rare occasions, and this is one of Pennsylvania's rarest breeding birds as they are sensitive to disturbance.

Medium build with a long body and a slender shape. Rufous-brown facial discs often look long, rather than round.

Short-eared Owl

Asio flammeus

L 15" | **WS** 37"

The Short-eared Owl is a phantom of the twilight hours, cruising marshes, meadows, and grassy fields like a giant moth. It floats with erratic wing beats, keeping low to the ground as it searches and swoops for mice and other small rodents. Sometimes even active during the day, it is most often seen foraging at dawn and dusk, but occasionally one is flushed from a roosting site in grassy or shrubby areas. It sometimes perches on high points like hay bales, telephone poles, and fence posts, and you can see that its ear tufts are small and very short, or they may not be apparent at all. While a few pairs breed in the state, nesting amid reclaimed strip mines in places such as Clarion County, most Short-eareds are seen between December and March. Migrants are also detected during the peaks of their northbound movement in April and when heading south in November.

Note tubular body, round face, long rounded wings. Underparts pale buff with streaky breast.

Ear tufts often not visible. Note dark eye sockets, whitish rim to the facial disk. Spotted buff and brown above.

Common Nighthawk

Chordeiles minor

L 9" | **WS** 21.5"

Known locally in some areas as the "bullbat" for its erratic bat-like flight and its twilight habits, the buzzy cry of the nighthawk is an emblematic sound of warm summer evenings. Its call is an insect-like *tzzzzzert,* given in flight as it bounds around over open ground, urban gravel rooftops, and along rivers searching for insects. An aerial insectivore, this bird is in the nightjar family, and despite the name is not related to hawks. The nighthawk flies both high and low with snappy wingbeats. Absent in winter, sightings are from May to September, with peak numbers on the southbound migration in August and September.

Marbled black, white, and gray. Long, pointed wings and short tail. Belly is barred.

Obvious white band in outer wing.

Eastern Whip-poor-will

Antrostomus vociferus

L 9.75" | **WS** 19"

Sitting silently on a branch or perfectly camouflaged amid leaf litter during the day, the Whip-poor-will stirs after the sun sets, bursting forth with is forceful call. The persistent rollicking cry for which it is named, a loud *Whip-rrrr WILL!* is a sound of summer nights, heard in open woodlands in much of the state. Absent in winter, it occurs here from April to September, with most sightings in May and June. By mid-July it becomes quieter and harder to detect. A true night bird, it is generally difficult to see, but at times it is spotted at night on roads when car headlights illuminate the eyes and reflect its eyeshine. Most often found in gaps in the forest, hunting moths and other flying insects, it sits on the ground or perches on a branch, staring up at the sky with its large, dark nocturnal eyes, and sallies up to grab its prey.

Broad gray stripe across shoulder and back. Males have bold white spots in outer tail. Females have smaller buff spots.

Chimney Swift
Chaetura pelagica

L 5.25" | **WS** 10.5-11.75"

Incredible aerialists, Chimney Swifts are rarely seen perched. In fact, they cannot really perch at all, but are adapted to nest and roost on sheer faces such as inside chimneys, abandoned smoke-stacks, or hollow trees. Nesting today almost exclusively in open-top chimneys, the twittering call of this bird is a positive sign of spring. Often referred to as a "flying cigar," the Chimney Swift is a fantastic migrant, wintering in South America, vanishing from the North American continent in November or earlier, and then storming back in April. The small Chimney Swift is usually seen hurtling through the sky with rapid, stiff wing-beats, changing directions abruptly, diving, and then steaming upward again. Usually where there is one, there are others. Swirling over our cities, towns, ponds, and any other patch of sky where there it finds food, it feeds on aerial plankton (tiny insects) within rising columns of air. It is widespread and common from May through September, but recent years have seen significant declines in their numbers, perhaps associated with the practice of capping chimneys and loss of industrial chimneys in many towns.

Soot-colored with long, thin swept-back wings. In September large roosts of hundreds or more occur in big chimneys.

Ruby-throated Hummingbird

Archilochus colubris

L 3–3.5" | **WS** 3–4.5"

A little green gem of a bird, the buzzy movements and tiny size of the Ruby-throated Hummingbird make it seem almost as much an insect as a bird. In fact, it is our smallest breeding bird, widespread from April into September, and common in a remarkable variety of habitats including forested creeks, parks, backyards, and other edge habitats. Though usually it is absent from the most populated parts of cities, in late summer and early fall some even wander into highly urban areas, feeding at window box flowers or similar arrangements with flowering plants. While famous for nectaring at flowers, the hummingbird also preys on small insects. Sometimes one is seen gathering spider webs as nesting material. Hummingbird feeders are marvelous for attracting several or more hummers to the backyard. Though Ruby-throateds typically depart for points south by mid-October, feeders kept full into late fall and beyond may attract rarer species of vagrant hummingbirds.

Adult male has a ruby throat ("gorget"), but this appears black at angles where it does not catch sunlight.

Female white below, with small black area on the lores and behind the eye. Upperparts emerald green like male.

Belted Kingfisher
Megaceryle alcyon

L 12.5" | **WS** 21"

The crazy crest and expressive nature of the kingfisher, make it a perpetual crowd-pleaser. Hanging out along creeks, rivers, and at the margins of large ponds and lakes, it is always near water and explodes onto the scene with a rollicking *kik-kik-kik-kik-kik* rattle. Taking a perch that offers good views of the water below, it sits until it spies its target. Hunting mostly small fish, the showy kingfisher hovers in place over the water, before plunging force-fully straight down into the water, making a splash and using its heavy bill to grab its prey. Present year-round nearly throughout the state, during spring and summer it nests in holes that it excavates out of bare dirt banks along edges of the water.

Grayish blue above with big head, and heavy dagger-like bill. Expressive crest becomes particularly spiky when the bird is excited. Male white below with single bluish breast band.

Female has rusty belt across breast.

Yellow-bellied Sapsucker

Sphyrapicus varius

L 7-8.75" | **WS** 13.5-16"

With its colorful name and unusual habit of drilling sap wells in trees, the sapsucker also differs from our other woodpeckers in its highly migratory nature. A medium-size woodpecker, the sapsucker breeds in boreal forests throughout the U.S. and Canada, and winters south through Central America. It is a common breeder in the expansive stretches of forest along the northern edge of the state, winters in much of the southern half of the state, and is seen widely during migration. Preferring open woodlands, migrants turn up even in urban areas with few trees, and neat horizontal rows of holes on a tree trunk are a tell-tale sign that a sapsucker has been around. Sapsuckers are fond of maples, birches, and aspens, and their sap wells are utilized also by hummingbirds and other insectivores. It is relatively quiet for a woodpecker, but listen for its mewing *khehh* call.

Adults have red on crown, boldly striped face. Male has red throat. Note bold white wing stripe and checkered back, featured also on dusky-headed juveniles.

Red-headed Woodpecker

Melanerpes erythrocephalus

L 9.25" | **WS** 17"

A dapper bird, unlike most of our other woodpeckers the Red-headed shows no spotting or barring and is our only woodpecker with an entirely red head. It is a mid-size woodpecker, at home in more open woodlands and swamps with a mix of live and dead trees, and is relatively quiet and inconspicuous, offering hoarse *wheer* or *cleah* calls interspersed with coughing churr sounds. Absent from the high plateau and the northeast, breeding occurs in the Piedmont, mountain valleys, and also in the northwest from Lawrence County north to the Lake Erie shore. It is scarce or rare in winter, and migrants are encountered in spring and especially in fall. It is nimble in flight, usually rather like a Blue Jay, and at times it hawks insects on the wing.

Distinctively patterned with black back and large white wing patch, white underparts and a white rump. Adults have a red hood.

Juvenile is gray-headed, but similar wing pattern to adult with gray-brown streaking on chest.

Red-bellied Woodpecker
Melanerpes carolinus

L 9.25" | **WS** 16"

A conspicuous resident of mixed and deciduous forests in most of the state, especially at lower elevations, the Red-bellied Woodpecker is one of our most widely encountered woodland birds. It is heard often, giving persistent coughing *chuh chuh, chuh* calls, and an exclamatory rattled *whurrr!* The eponymous red belly patch is seldom visible and hard to see. A regular visitor to bird feeders and backyards year-round, the Red-bellied hitches its way up tree trunks in search of insects; diet also includes acorns. It bursts into flight when startled, audibly flapping its wings and revealing pale patches in the outer wing.

Zebra-striped back, white rump, and red crown. Forehead and forecrown of female (pictured here) are gray; red crown extends forward on forehead to bill in male.

Downy Woodpecker

Picoides pubescens

L 6" | **WS** 11"

Our smallest woodpecker, the Downy is one of the most wide-spread and commonly encountered birds in Pennsylvania. From remote woodlands to backyards to urban situations with only scattered trees, this spirited woodpecker is one of our most conspicuous and vocal birds. Its common calls include a high-pitched descending whinny-rattle and an abrupt *tsik* or *pik*. These sounds are regular features of mixed songbird flocks in winter, where the Downy keeps company with chickadees, titmice, and other songbirds. When mingling with a mixed flock, it makes shorter flights from tree to tree within the forest. On longer flights in open space, it moves with the typical undulating woodpecker flight style, interspersing rising bouts of rapid wing beats with sinking close-winged glides.

Note large white patch on back, black-and-white checkered wings, and short, thin bill. Male has red patch on rear of crown.

Hairy Woodpecker

Picoides villosus

L 8.5" | **WS** 14.5"

A medium-size black-and-white woodpecker with a moderately long bill, the Hairy Woodpecker is like a huskier, heftier version of the Downy Woodpecker. The Hairy is relatively shy, however, and is choosier about where it spends its time, preferring larger woodlots with older trees. It forages mostly on mid-size or larger trees, and is found at times in suburban situations where older trees are present, but is always outnumbered by the more approachable Downy. The two differ in voice as well, and Hairy gives a loud explosive *kik!* or *keek!* This sound frequently precedes its longer call which is a raspy, even-pitched, chattering rattle. In flight its wingbeats are audible and quite loud, given its size.

Longer, heftier, and scarcer version of the more common Downy Woodpecker, with a noticeably longer and stronger bill. Male has red patch on rear of crown, which female lacks.

Northern Flicker

Colaptes auratus

L 11.5" | **WS** 18"

The flicker's odd conglomeration of unusual plumage features and its habit of foraging on the ground are unlike other woodpeckers. It is a relatively large for a woodpecker, and it can be rather social at times, and several or more may gather in a tree-top and make *flicka-flicka-flicka* sounds to one another. Quite vocal, its more common sound, given even when few others birds are calling, is a cry of *cleeah*. Like other woodpeckers, the flicker drums on trees to notify rivals that it has established its territory. Year-round residents across most of the state, they are also conspicuous migrants and on some days (especially in autumn) they stage noticeable flights, when one seems to bounce into view every few minutes throughout the day.

Mostly tan-brown; black bib; neatly spotted below. Male has black moustachial stripe; both sexes have red patch on rear of crown.

Relatively large; yellow in underwings obvious in flight; note white rump.

Pileated Woodpecker

Dryocopus pileatus

L 17.5" | **WS** 27.5"

A big, heavy woodpecker with a crow-like flight, the Pileated's large size and crimson crest are a startlingly regal combination. A widespread year-round resident, it does not lack for voice and its far-carrying cries are heard frequently in the mature stands of trees it prefers. It cries out regularly amid the older trees where it makes its home, and its sounds include an alarming, clear, resonant, and high-pitched *KAK-kak-kak-kak* and a lower, slower set of *wuk* notes, strung together. Territorial birds hammer their bill against a tree to make a loud, deep drumming sound that speeds up before fading out, and the drumming of the Pileated is much stronger than that of other woodpeckers.

Mostly black with white on neck, wrist, and underwing. Male has red cheek patch. Female has speckled dark forehead.

American Kestrel

Falco sparverius

L 10.5" | **WS** 22"

A petite bird of prey, the American Kestrel hunts mice and large insects in open areas, farm fields, and urban areas. It is most often seen perched on wires or posts along country roads. Like other falcons, it is dynamic on the wing, and it is often seen hovering over potential prey, looking straight down. This is our smallest falcon, with a relatively long tail and narrow pointed wings, features easily appreciated when seen in flight. Many kestrels pass through during their peaks of migration in March and April, and from September through October. The kestrel breeds and winters here in good numbers. Nests are found widely across the state in old woodpecker holes and in nest boxes, farm buildings, and abandoned buildings. When startled or excited, it lets loose with its shrill *kuh-lee kuh-lee kuh-lee kuh-lee kuh-lee* call.

Small and fidgety, with reddish back and tail, and pale face with dark vertical stripes. Rufous back is barred with black. Male has bluish gray wings.

Merlin

Falco columbarius

L 10.5" | **WS** 47.5"

A wonderful menace, few birds so visibly strike fear into the hearts of songbirds and small shorebirds as does the sleek, smart Merlin. Compact and cloaked in dark plumage, it moves with great purpose, speed, and agility, at times like a bullet and at others like a shadow. A fierce mid-size falcon, it prefers open areas with exposed perches. Unlike its larger cousin, the Peregrine Falcon, the Merlin attacks horizontally rather than from above. Most conspicuous in fall migration from September into December, it is also seen widely if uncommonly in winter. Look for it along the Lake Erie shore and at hawk-watching sites on the ridges such as at Hawk Mountain Sanctuary. The Merlin is a rare breeding bird in Pennsylvania, and several nests were recently discovered in northern counties, mostly in conifers

Dark overall, with solidly dark gray or gray-brown upperparts.

Note compact form and how the buff undertail contrasts with heavily streaked underparts.

Peregrine Falcon
Falco peregrinus

L 16.5" | **WS** 41"

Famous as the fastest bird in the world, the Peregrine Falcon is captivating when it is wheeling in the air, and as you catch its commanding gaze while it is perched. With streamlined, tapered wings, it moves with incredible speed, power and agility, chasing down shorebirds, small ducks, and doves, using dramatic stooping dives to snatch its prey. These spectacular spiraling dives sometimes reach speeds up to 200 miles per hour! By about 1960 the Peregrine had disappeared from Pennsylvania because of pesticide contamination, but reintroduction efforts beginning in the 1970s have established Peregrines as breeders in Pittsburgh, Harrisburg, Philadelphia, and elsewhere. Nesting on tall buildings, bridges, and cliffs, they often hunt near water, and are enjoyed frequently in spring and summer by city residents. The state also hosts migrant Peregrines that breed in Arctic nesting areas and pass through in migration, particularly in September and October. They concentrate along mountain ridges and shorelines as they move south.

Adults slaty above, with dark hood and mask, white breast, and barred underparts. Tapered wing shape is most noticeable during gliding or soaring.

Juvenile heavily marked below with dark streaking, including breast; darker overall than adult. Front of head paler and moustache narrower than adult.

Adult's back is steely bluish. Yellow around the eye, nostril, and legs.

Eastern Wood-Pewee
Contopus virens

L 6.25"　|　**WS** 10"

Alert and conspicuous in forested areas throughout the state from May to September, the wood-pewee is named for its sorrowful song, an oft-heard sound of summer: a drawn-out, somber *pee-uh-weee,* often followed by a shorter *see-boo*. (Starlings regularly mimic the song). Singing from exposed perches within woodlands, the wood-pewee is vocal and active on even the hottest afternoons, sitting on snags of the mid- or upper story of the forest. It sallies up to snag bugs, at times audibly snapping its bill shut on an insect, before returning to a favorite perch and quivering its tail in rapid sideways movements. Famous for foraging from the same perch, flying out and returning to it again and again.

Note upright posture, long wings, short legs. Face dusky with weak eye ring. Smudgy vest on breast; narrow pale grayish wing bars.

Eastern Phoebe

Sayornis phoebe

L 7" | **WS** 10.5"

The phoebe is a hearty insectivore, more tolerant of cold than other flycatchers. Plump and long-tailed, the phoebe is confiding and alert, routinely pumping its tail up as it rests at a perch. Preferring the lower or mid-story of wooded areas near water. It breeds across the state in shady woodlots near lakes or ponds, in semi-open forests, and even forested backyards, nesting under the eaves of small buildings and houses, under bridges, and on rocky ledges. Adults on breeding territories sing a cheerful *Sree-beh! Fee abit-it* sometimes offering only the first phrase, the sound for which it is named. The call note is a sweet, chipper *tsip,* heard especially in migration when phoebes frequent parks, margins of brushy thickets, and edges of woodlands near a pond or lake. Found widely from March into November, numbers dwindle such that it is rare in winter, when it is seen mainly in the southeast.

Charcoal upperparts, dark head, wing bars absent or faint. Dark smudge on sides of breast; creamy below. Juvenile yellowish on belly.

Acadian Flycatcher

Empidonax virescens

L 5.75" | **WS** 9"

With a medium build and drab plumage, the Acadian Flycatcher's most distinctive features are its call and its preference for dark, dank woodlands. Preferring swampy forests, streams shaded by broadleaf trees, or hemlock ravines, it stays near the water or calls from the upper story of the forest, belting out its explosive song, an emphatic *peet-za!* The Acadian resembles all other *Empidonax* flycatchers, but it is more retiring in its habits, usually keeping to areas within the forest. It is present here from May to September and is a strong flier, migrating to South America for the winter. Breeding across much of the state, it is most conspicuous in spring and early summer when it is singing to establish its territory.

Similar to other *Empidonax*, but larger, greener, with long wings and relatively large, broad bill. Also shows a thin whitish eye ring.

Alder and Willow Flycatchers

Empidonax alnorum / Empidonax tailli

L 6" │ **WS** 8.5"

The Alder Flycatcher and the Willow Flycatcher (*Empidonax traillii*) are essentially identical in appearance and were once considered a single species. Distibguished by voice, the Willow Flycatcher has a sneezy *fitz-bew* advertising song, but keeps contact with its mate with a thin upward *wit!* Alder's song is a reedy *free beer!* and its contact note is a husky, flat *kep!* Both species winter in the tropics, and are present here from May to September. The Willow is generally more common and breeds across the state, nesting in shrubs in open fields and along streams. The Alder often inhabits swamps and alder thickets, and the two species sometimes occupy territories within a few feet of each other. The more northerly Alder is a slightly later migrant and nests more commonly in the northern half of the state and at higher elevations.

The Alder (pictured here) and Willow Flycatchers are identical in appearance, both flat-headed, and grayish brown-olive.

Least Flycatcher
Empidonax minimus

L 5.25" | **WS** 7.75"

A petite flycatcher favoring open patches in forest understory, the Least is a regular migrant and breeding bird here. Present from May to September, it nests in the Allegheny Mountains and across the northern half of the state. It occurs as a migrant elsewhere during spring and fall. It nests usually in mixed or deciduous forest, and woodland edge, and when calling, it can scarcely go unnoticed. The loud *tse-beck* call is unlike other *Empidonax,* and is often repeated again and again. Migrants are less vocal when found in hedgerows and brushy thickets, and are best distinguished by size and shape. Look for them in forests of northern counties including Loyalsock State Forest, State Game Lands 12 in Bradford County, around Elk State Forest, and in Allegheny National Forest.

Our smallest flycatcher; note relatively big head, with noticeable pale eye ring. Wing tips are short. Tail differs from other flycatchers in being both short and narrow.

Yellow-bellied Flycatcher

Empidonax flaviventris

L 5-6" | **WS** 7-8"

With good alert posture and relatively bright plumage for an *Empidonax,* this is a nice-looking flycatcher, but one that is not easy to find. It prefers to remain low within shady, brushy stands or the understory of dense coniferous woods, and keeps a low profile. The Yellow-bellied does not announce itself as loudly as some flycatchers, delivering its typical *ts-bick* song at a leisurely pace of 6 to 10 times a minute. In contrast, the Least Flycatcher's song is delivered at a frantic pace. The Yellow-bellied's short *tsu-ee* call note is easily overlooked, but is frequently given in migration. It nests in the state in small numbers on the high plateau, such as in Sullivan and Wyoming counties, but is mostly seen during migration in the second half of May or in September. Watch for it low in the dark recesses of woodlots, hunting warily beneath the canopy, flitting from branch to branch, snatching insects as it moves.

Olive breast, yellowish in throat and belly. Olive cheeks contrast little with the throat; pale wing bars contrast strongly with black wings. Shows distinct pale eye ring.

Great Crested Flycatcher

Myiarchus crinitus

L 8.75" | **WS** 13"

Even on the hottest summer afternoons when scarcely another bird is found, the Great Crested Flycatcher remains active, hunting large insects in the woodland canopy, and calling frequently. Its explosive loud *Weep!* is also incorporated into the boisterous song, which is a rolling set of *werp* noises mixed with other staccato notes. Though it possesses a conspicuous voice, it often remains within the treetops, hunting in mid- or upper stories, making it hard to see at times. It is particularly fond of semi-open woodlots, and is common throughout the state from May to September. Similar flycatchers discovered after October should be scrutinized for the possibility of a rare, look-alike Ash-throated Flycatcher. Unlike our other flycatchers, the Great Crested nests in tree cavities and woodpecker holes. It often decorates the nest with shed snake skin.

Large with heavy bill, yellow belly, gray chest, reddish in wings and tail. Brownish above.

Eastern Kingbird

Tyrannus tyrannus

L 9" | **WS** 15"

Our largest flycatcher, the simply patterned kingbird is a conspicuous part of the summer scene, perching on wires in open spaces and edge habitats. Sitting with its horizontal posture, it waits for an insect to fly into view and then sallies out, snatching at it sometimes with an audible snap of the bill. At other times it is seen in hot pursuit of a crow, vulture, or hawk, hounding it relentlessly around the head and back, and issuing a bewildering array of kingbird expletives. It is for this aggressive and territorial and tyrannical behavior that it is given its English and scientific names. From May to September, this is one of the state's most widespread birds, calling frequently with a shrill, buzzy *t-t-tzzzzee, or tzeeer.*

Black above, pale whitish below with crisp, narrow white tail band. Often shows dusky chest. When aroused or furious, a tiny red crown patch is sometimes visible.

Northern Shrike
Lanius excubitor

L 8.5" | **WS** 12"

Sneaky shrikes superficially resemble a mockingbird, but in fact are predatory songbirds. Known locally in places as "butcherbirds" or "nine-killers," shrikes are alert, alluring, and brutal birds, famous for their habit of impaling small birds, rodents, and large insects on thorns or barbed wire. They hunt along hedgerows and thickets adjacent to open fields or meadows, using wires overhead or other exposed perches. The Northern Shrike is an uncommon or rare winter visitor and requires a special effort to see—an observer is very lucky to discover one. Another species of shrike, the Loggerhead Shrike (*Lanius ludovicianus*), breeds on occasion in Franklin and Adams counties, but is otherwise only a very rare visitor to the state.

Note hooked bill, used for tearing into prey; pale pearly gray, with small pale area at base of bill, narrow black mask, and thin white eye ring. Fine grayish barring below.

White-eyed Vireo

Vireo griseus

L 5" | **WS** 7.5"

Spunky, colorful, and a spirited songster, the White-eyed Vireo is a common nesting bird in the southeastern and western parts of the state. Present from April to September, it favors dense understory, scrubby thickets, and viny tangles in edge habitat. Often it remains hidden in vegetation, foraging for insects or fruit, but like other vireos, it is vocal and sings throughout the day. Both males and females sing, and routinely incorporate (mimic) call notes of other birds into their own song. Common song types include an exclamatory *Spit-TEER veh-VEER check!* or an abrupt "Shaaave an'a haircut!" Alert and feisty, it is not uncommon to hear the White-eyed scolding potential predators or other perceived nuisances with harsh scratchy calls.

Adult has white eyes with yellow "goggles," yellow flanks, white wing bars, gray neck, and greenish back. Juvenile has dark eyes, lacks yellow on face.

Yellow-throated Vireo

Vireo flavifrons

L 5.5" | **WS** 9.5"

The Yellow-throated is one of the most strikingly plumaged vireos. Keeping to the upper story of closed-canopy larger deciduous trees, it moves relatively sluggishly from branch to branch, calling often. Its simple song is lackadaisical, a set of two or three burry phrases, repeated and commonly described as "three, eight" or perhaps *cheerio... jeereer... jibber.* It is more easily found by listening than by visual searching. It delivers a scratchy series of scold notes when agitated. Present from May to September, in migration it is sometimes found in scrubby or brushy woodland or edge habitat, but is more often seen in semi-open deciduous woodlands, including along creeks and rivers. It breeds across much of Pennsylvania, nesting in older tracts of forest, especially those containing oaks and maples, where it hunts for caterpillars.

Bright yellow chest contrasts sharply with bright white belly. Note yellow spectacles, green head and neck, and gray back with pale wing bars.

Blue-headed Vireo

Vireo solitarius

L 5.5" | **WS** 9.5"

Dapper and confiding, the Blue-headed Vireo is a welcome sight.
Moving about deliberately in the mid-story of the forest, it is seen
singly or among a mixed flock of woodland birds including
chickadees and kinglets. A common breeder and migrant, it occurs
mostly from April to October, but being more tolerant of cold than
other vireos, sometimes arrives earlier or lingers later. It nests
throughout the mountains and the plateau, preferring mixed
woodlands or stands of evergreens, especially hemlock. Migrants
occur widely in a variety of woodlands, or sometimes brushy
habitats, where they hunt for insects or pick fruit in the mid- and
upper story. Like other vireos, the Blue-headed is vocal, and most
easily detected by voice. It seems to talk to itself and answer
stringing together clear, liquid phrases. Listen and look for it in
Allegheny National Forest, Loyalsock State Forest, State Game
Lands 13 and 57, or at Ricketts Glen State Park.

White spectacles and white
throat contrast with gray
head. Back green, flanks are
rich green or yellow-green.

Warbling Vireo

Vireo gilvus

L 4.5" | **WS** 8.75"

Not our showiest bird, the Warbling Vireo is perhaps most noteworthy for its song. The wheezy, rising, meandering warble is heard not just during dawn choruses, but also in the heat of the mid-day sun in summer. Wintering in Central America, it is present here as a migrant and breeder from April to September, and is strongly tied to our rivers and creeks. It nests in syca-mores, silver maples, and cottonwoods in both cities and rural areas, and methodically hunts caterpillars and insects in the mid- and upper stories.

Pale gray overall, with blank expression and dark eye. Darker crown is offset by paler eyebrow; most show faint darkish line through eye.

Philadelphia Vireo

Vireo philadelphicus

L 5.25" | **WS** 8"

Named by legendary ornithologist John Cassin (from Delaware County, Pennsylvania) because the first known specimen was from Philadelphia, this vireo is not easily seen in the state. Breeding to our north and wintering in Central America, it occurs only as an uncommon migrant during narrow time spans in May and September. It is usually seen hunting insects or taking fruit in deciduous forests, mixed semi-open woodlands, or in brushy edge habitat. In May, it is more easily found west of the mountains, but can still be hard to find. These vireos do not sing much en route, and even then sound very similar to Red-eyed Vireos. In fall, they occur more widely, including in the southeast, and often join mixed flocks. Probably they are often overlooked, being relatively quiet and resembling the far more common Warbling Vireo.

Often confused with Warbling Vireo, but slightly smaller proportions, dark lores, darker crown, and yellowish throat. Gray crown contrasts sharply with white eyebrow.

Red-eyed Vireo

Vireo olivaceus

L 6" | **WS** 10"

Abundant in woodlands in summer, the Red-eyed Vireo works
within treetops, favoring sunlit gaps in the canopy where it sings
endlessly throughout the day. From May through July its whistled
song is routinely heard on woodland walks across the state. The
song is a series of short, hustled, melodic, sing-song phrases of
three or four notes, given in steady succession "See me up here?
Don't I look sweet? Yes I see you. You're not so sweet." Wintering in
South America, the Red-eyed Vireo is here from May to October.
Migrants can frequent brushy woodlands or tall hedgerows that
separate open areas, most often they prefer forest and woodland
edge with a mix of tall conifers and hardwoods containing some
good understory cover. They often join mixed flocks of woodland
birds, but otherwise hunt caterpillars and other insects in the
mid- or upper story of the forest.

Greenish above, pearly white
below, with white throat. Gray
crown with dark eye line on
each side of white eyebrow.
Long, strong bill. In autumn,
juveniles have a brown eye.

Blue Jay

Cyanocitta cristata

L 11" | **WS** 16"

The nifty and jazzy Blue Jay bursts with personality, sporting a stylish and expressive blue crest and a black necklace. Social and chatty, they are common year-round, frequenting backyards and woodland areas, often keeping near oaks where they take acorns. Jays prefer deciduous or mixed woodlands, and become raucous and loud if they find a roosting owl or hawk, mobbing it with crows or other songbirds. In the same family as crows and ravens, the Blue Jay is adaptable, intelligent, and capable of a remarkable array of sounds. Famous for mimicking hawk calls, especially the Red-shouldered Hawk, the typical call is an often a repeated, hoarse *jay*. They also can sound like a squeaky wheel or a pump handle when excited. Jays are understandably less noisy and more retiring during the nesting season in summer, but become conspicuous again in fall when migrating, moving during the day in loose flocks, and calling frequently. Blue Jays cache food including acorns, inadvertently planting many trees.

Unique plumage pattern, mostly blue with black barring and white spots in wings and tail. Black collar is variable in shape and pattern. Crest is flattened at rest and when foraging, but erected when agitated.

Fish Crow
Corvus ossifragus

L 15" │ **WS** 36"

The Fish Crow is best known by its throaty, nasal voice. The distinctive call is a pessimistic-sounding *unh-uh* or *eh-eh*. Compared to the very similar and more widespread American Crow, the Fish Crow is more a bird of rivers and valleys, and frequents landfills and agricultural areas. Common in the southeast, its range stretches north along the rivers and into mountain valleys. It occurs in modest numbers around Pittsburgh, but it is absent from areas of high elevation west of the Allegheny Front. Look for it along the Delaware River Trail in Philadelphia, along the lower Susquehanna River, and at Frick Park in Pittsburgh. Hundreds occur around landfills in Bucks County.

Nearly identical to American Crow, but smaller and glossier, with more rounded wings in flight. Best identified by voice. Usually less skittish and more confiding than American Crow.

American Crow

Corvus brachyrhynchos

L 18.5" | **WS** 36.5"

The crafty and clever American Crow is a truly fascinating bird. Common year-round in a range of habitats from expansive woodlands to small patches of forest, agricultural areas, and suburban and even urban areas, the crow is at home almost anywhere so long as there are a few good high perches. The ultimate omnivore, it subsists on a wide array of foods, including fruit, seeds, roadkill, and garbage. It also raids the nests of other birds, taking eggs or young. Highly intelligent and resourceful, crows may live long lives and have a complex social structure, amassing in huge winter roosts, and in summer working together in family groups to raise young. Remarkably adaptable, the crow is also the owner of an intriguing array of sounds, and in addition to the common *caw,* it emits a mix of croaks and rattles.

In flight, smaller than raven, with rounded tail and shorter wings and shorter, smaller bill. Compare with similar, smaller Fish Crow. Crows seem to row in the air. Large, stout, with solid black plumage, medium-length bill.

Common Raven

Corvus corax

L 24.5" | **WS** 46"

The imposing, impressive raven is one of the most widespread birds in the Northern Hemisphere, and the largest songbird in the world. Its range is expanding in Pennsylvania. A year-round resident across our high plateau and mountains, it has traditionally been scarce in the southeast and much of the central-west, but today this nomadic bird is detected at more and more new locations in these areas. Good spots to see it include Ricketts Glen State Park, State Game Lands 13 and 57, Loyalsock State Forest, World's End State Park, and Black Moshannon State Park. Ravens often soar, like a large raptor, and they are generally more dynamic in the air, engaging in rolls and dives. Voice is helpful in identifying black corvids, and ravens issue a remarkable variety of sounds including an urgent, loud, throaty, croaking *raaah* that is often repeated again and again.

Large, heavy black bird, with long, heavy bill and long wings. Strong legs and feet. In flight, note how wedge-shaped tail tapers to a point in the middle. Head projects far ahead of body.

Horned Lark

Eremophila alpestris

L 7" | **WS** 12.5"

From farm fields to airports and golf courses to reclaimed strip mines, the Horned Lark is an open-country bird, common across much of the state. Although widespread year-round and often in flocks, it can be overlooked because of its flighty nature, pale plumage, and subtle call notes. Well-camouflaged, Horned Larks feed unobtrusively in sparsely vegetated fields, where their voice often gives them away. They are attracted to bare ground in harvested corn fields and manure spreads. Careful listening along country roads at margins of fields should result in hearing their thin wispy notes and chirps, especially as they pick up and fly. In spring and summer they sing, producing a pleasant song that begins with a handful of staccato *tsert tsit* chirps and finishes with a rapid series of rougher jumbled notes all running together.

Sandy or clay brown back, whitish underparts. "Horns" often not visible even at close range, but note yellowish throat and black bars on crown, face and neck.

Northern Rough-winged Swallow

Stelgidopteryx serripennis

L 5" | **WS** 11"

Brownish overall with a floaty flight, the Rough-winged is at home along rivers, creeks, and lake edges. Nesting in cavities such as woodpecker holes, pipes, crevices in trees, man-made structures, and in riverbanks, this swallow breeds throughout the state. Mostly present from April into October, a rather startling discovery was that it has over-wintered in Philadelphia for the last decade or so, subsisting on insects at a wastewater treatment plant along the Delaware River. This is the only known wintering population for hundreds of miles around. The Rough-winged may consort with other swallows, but on the wing it moves with relatively deliberate, airy, rowing wingbeats compared to the others, and it often calls, emitting *frip* notes that it repeats in fits and starts.

Brown above with pale brown chest, whiter belly. Flight action slightly different from other swallows. Smaller Bank Swallow also has brown back.

In flight, note broad wings and low contrast between belly and chest (though chest is peachy on juveniles). White undertail coverts sometimes visible from above.

Bank Swallow

Riparia riparia

L 5" | **WS** 10.5"

Our smallest swallow, the Bank Swallow darts about with quick, jerky wingbeats, whether high in the sky or low over a river or a field. A social and nimble aerialist, it is present from April through September. Migrants occur widely and often forage with other swallows, especially at lakes and along waterways. It breeds at scattered sites across the state in small colonies where the birds dig nest holes into riverbanks, quarries, and bluffs. Colonies may suddenly appear one spring only to vanish the next as banks and bluffs erode and quarry walls are altered. The call is a quiet, reedy *rip*, repeated intermittently.

Small, brown-backed with narrow, pointed wings and brown band across breast.

Purple Martin
Progne subis

L 8" | **WS** 16"

Our largest and most migratory swallow, this charismatic, social, aerial insectivore is an early migrant. Vanishing to South America for the winter, martins return in early or mid-April, ushering in the spring season before most other migrant birds have yet returned. Breeding especially in the southeast and northwest of the state, the martin also nests in the mountains and valleys. Nearly all nests today are built in man-made houses or nesting gourds around suburban homes or farmhouses. They remain into September. Alert listeners often hear martins before seeing them, as they offer assertive *churt* or *dzeep* notes, and often mix in an odd crack and rattle.

Males are deep glossy purple overall.

Female and juvenile have dark head and back, grayish breast and neck, pale belly.

Tree Swallow

Tachycineta bicolor

L 5.25" | **WS** 13"

The Tree Swallow is one of our most common and conspicuous aerial insectivores. Careening on broad triangular wings, they intersperse longer glides with bouts of choppy flapping, ascending up and gliding down. Looping with erratic movements, they hawk tiny insects over fields, wetlands, and other open areas near water, calling as they go. The common call is a chirping *skip-it,* repeated again and again; also mellow *tsoo-it* phrases. Present mostly from March to November, Tree Swallows breed commonly across much of the state, readily accepting nest boxes for roosting and breeding, and nesting in old woodpecker holes. Though rare in winter, they are generally more tolerant of cold than most other swallows, and are among the first migrants to return and the latest to linger. In late summer and autumn, they gather in flocks for roosting and feeding, and sometimes are seen by the thousands.

Adult male (and some females) are blue above and clean white below.

Female (pictured) and juvenile are dark-backed, and white below. Juveniles in late summer or fall sometimes show faint grayish on chest.

Barn Swallow

Hirundo rustica

L 6.5" | **WS** 12"

Small, sleek, and slender, the Barn Swallow's long, forked tail makes it unlike other swallows. Foraging in open areas, it hawks small insects on the wing, zipping around over ball fields, large lawns, agricultural fields, wetlands, and water bodies. Often it keeps low to the ground, but especially in migration or during really hot days, it may forage high in the air, joining other swallows and swifts. Absent in winter, it is one of our most common songbirds from April until October. Named for its affinity for nesting in open barns, it also affixes its nest of straw and mud under eaves, inside porches or gazebos, and in other buildings. Seldom is a nest not attached to a man-made structure. To rest, the Barn Swallow perches on wires, docks, wooden railings, or thin leafless branches. Its calls are cheerful and yappy, often in a rapid-fire series, but sometimes are single *djeep* or *jip* notes.

Bluish above and tawny brown below, with brown forehead and breast. Tail may appear pointed when closed.

Cliff Swallow

Petrochelidon pyrrhonota

L 5" | **WS** 11.5"

The compact Cliff Swallow is best known for its social nesting habits, breeding in colonies under bridges, on dams, in gazebos, and pavilions. Groups of these dapper, chunky swallows swarm around man-made structures, constructing round nests from mud they carry in their mouth. Nests have a neat circular entrance/exit on the side where the birds can be seen poking their heads out. Nesting across much of the Allegheny plateau, and in the mountains and valleys, it is less common as a breeding bird in the southeast and southwest, but is widespread as a migrant. Arriving in mid-April and departing in mid-September, the Cliff Swallow seems to favor following waterways and ridges in migration. Late-fall or early-winter birds should be carefully compared with the similar but rare Cave Swallow.

Stocky, with short, square tail, pale buff or cinnamon rump, white forehead, and black throat. Belly is pale whitish.

Carolina Chickadee

Poecile carolinensis

L 4.75" | **WS** 7.5"

Confiding, spirited little sprites of forests, thickets, parks and
woodlots, chickadees are common visitors to backyards and bird
feeders across the state. Present here year-round, they stick to
treed areas, and typically are found in small groups or leading
mixed species feeding flocks, and their sounds give them away.
When agitated they give a series of rapid high-pitched *tsee* notes,
but just as often one hears their namesake *tsk a dee dee dee* call.
The song is a sing-song *see-boo see-bay*. This bird is very similar
to the Black-capped Chickadee, and the two interbreed across
much of the southern third of the state. Absent from the northern
half of the state and high-elevation areas, where it is replaced by
Black-capped, Carolina is confined to the southeast and the
southwest. Typical adults are slightly smaller than Black-capped,
with a smaller head, and a neater and smaller black bib, but the
two are best distinguished by voice. The songs differ and Carolina's *chick-a-dee* call is faster paced and higher pitched.

Small with gray body and black and
white head. Compare with similar
Black-capped Chickadee. Carolina has
small head, neat black bib; grayish at
rear of cheeks; wing coverts are gray,
though some have pale gray edging.

Black-capped Chickadee

Poecile atricapillus

L 5.5" | **WS** 7.75"

One of our most familiar backyard birds, this dapper little chickadee is undeniably cute. Common in treed areas in the plateau and highlands in the center and north of the state, the chickadee is curious and inquisitive. Traveling through woodlots, thickets and parks in small groups, they visit feeders, or fly in to check out hikers or dog-walkers. If they find an owl, snake, cat or other predator, they fuss and scold, kicking up a stir and attracting other songbirds to join the mob. They dangle upside down while extracting seeds and fruit from tree branches, and make charming, chatty sounds. In addition to the *chick-a-dee* calls, the common song is a mellow, two-noted *tsee-bee*. Mostly the Black-capped is absent from the coastal plain, visiting the state's southernmost corners in winter. It is locally common or uncommon in the southwest and the Piedmont.

Gray and white body with black and white head. Compared to similar Carolina, Black-capped is heavier, bull-headed, has a longer tail, more extensive black bib that is messy at the corners, and extensive white in wing coverts.

Tufted Titmouse

Baeolophus bicolor

L 6.5" | **WS** 9.5"

The titmouse is common year-round in treed areas, often visiting backyard bird feeders, as well as forests, woodlots, and parks. Usually in pairs, they keep company with chickadees, and attend mixed feeding flocks with kinglets, nuthatches, and woodpeckers as they move through the trees in search of food. Subsisting on fruit, seeds and insects, the titmouse may forage in the upper canopy of a woodland or on the lawn below a bush, but is always near cover. Nesting in tree cavities and old woodpecker holes, behaviorally it is similar to the smaller chickadees and, like them, is vocal. It gives a grating scold when it detects a disturbance, and its *peter, peter, peter* song is among the most commonly heard sounds of the forest.

Gray with buff flanks, black forehead, and obvious crest. Big black doe eye.

Brown Creeper

Certhia americana

L 5" | **WS** 7.25"

Tiny and slender, this well-named woodland bird is unobtrusive, as it quietly scoots up a tree trunk. Working up and up, it moves along the trunk and sometimes out along larger tree branches before flying down to a new tree trunk to start upward again. It is shy and will hitch to the other side of the tree when approached, spiraling up the trunk. As it hunts for insects and spiders amid bark in this fashion, it is inconspicuous. Unlike birds of the winter flocks it feeds with (such as chickadees, nuthatches, and kinglets), the call easily slips by unnoticed. It is a quiet, thin, one-syllable, high-pitched ringing note, and at breeding areas it sings a longer, high-pitched "seeeee, look at me up here," with the first and last notes thin and ringing, like the call. A year-round resident, the creeper breeds in coniferous woods in the northern half of the state, and winters widely.

Small, slender, fluffy, and brown, note the slender pointed bill. Buffy wing stripe noticeable in flight.

Red-breasted Nuthatch

Sitta canadensis

L 4.25" | **WS** 7.5"

Absurdly cute and active, the strikingly patterned Red-breasted Nuthatch is an eye-catching little bird. It exhibits fidgety movements as it searches for food. Like so many songbirds, it feeds mostly upon insects in summer and switches to a diet of seeds and fruit in winter. Suet feeders attract them, too. Almost always they stay within conifers, especially pines and spruces, but also in mixed woodlands, hitching up tree trunks and around branches, calling often. The nasal *yank* call has a honking quality, vaguely reminiscent of the beeping sound a large truck makes as it reverses. Breeding in the northern half of the state, it winters and migrates throughout, but numbers vary from year to year. In some autumns after a successful breeding season, Red-breasteds stage "invasions," when large numbers are suddenly evident in migration and into winter, but in other years few are found.

Strongly patterned black-and-white head and buff-orange underparts.

White-breasted Nuthatch

Sitta carolinensis

L 5.25" | **WS** 9.25"

Known locally as "devil downhead" for its habit of descending
tree trunks head-first, the squat, chesty White-breasted
Nuthatch is the larger of our two nuthatches. A widespread
resident throughout the state, this nuthatch prefers large,
mature deciduous trees, in woodlands, parks, and backyards in
suburban and rural settings. Using its long, sturdy, upturned
bill, it pokes and probes into tree bark, in search of spiders and
insects. It is also attracted to feeders (especially suet cakes) and
is known for shoving seeds and nuts into tree bark and then
hacking away at them with the bill to open them up. Considering
their small size, nuthatches are surprisingly noisy, and the
White-breasted is often heard before it is seen, giving nasal *yank*
and *heh* notes.

White face, with extensive
black on top of head, and
long bill. Pale below, with
rusty undertail feathers.

House Wren

Troglodytes aedon

L 4.75" | **WS** 6"

The warbling, rolling, chattering song of the House Wren is an undeniable sign of spring. Heard in backyards, thickets, edge habitats, and parks in suburban and rural areas across the state from April through October, this little bird is tough and pugnacious. Driving out other species from potential nest sites, the House Wren is known to spoil nests of others birds deemed competitors, even ruining their eggs and young. Nesting in cracks, holes, or crevices in trees and commonly making use of nest boxes, it is a widespread migrant and breeding bird. Conspicuous in spring and summer due to the boisterous song and nesting habits, autumn migrants more often fly under the radar. In general, House Wrens prefer to stay within cover in brushy hedgerows, low viny tangles, and other dense under-story habitat, but they can be heard giving scratchy *cherr* or *tet* scold notes.

Gray-brown overall, long tail compared to other wrens, and plain face. Bill is horn-colored at base. Pale unmarked gray-brown underparts. Cavity-nesting, territorial species that regularly makes use of nest boxes.

Winter Wren

Troglodytes hiemalis

L 3.5" | **WS** 4.75-6.25"

Stub-tailed and alert, this tiny, fussy bird is our smallest wren, but what it lacks in size it makes up for in voice. The long, meandering, twittering song is spectacular, making this wren one of our most accomplished songsters. Nesting within expanses of dank, dark forest (especially hemlock) in the mountains and the plateau, it is most at home along creeks and streams where there are fallen logs with thick understory, roots and tangles. They also frequent boggy areas and rocky slopes, and in migration take to thickets and brush piles. With mouse-like movements, they hardly seem to fly so much as to dart and scurry within the understory, and they are more easily heard than seen. Away from breeding areas, the most commonly heard call is an agitated *dip dip* or *dup dup dup*. Look for it in the highlands of the Allegheny National Forest and in Loyalsock State Forest.

Tiny, and dark brown with thin dark bill, a pale eyebrow, and short tail. Stubbier and rounder than House Wren, and heavily barred on the undertail.

Marsh Wren

Cistothorus palustris

L 4.75" | **WS** 6.75"

With its expressive tail cocked up over its back as it straddles cattails, the Marsh Wren is a wren of wetlands. Like so many marsh birds, is active both at night and during the day. The rattling, burbling song is a regular feature of large, reedy marshes in the southeast and northwest from May through October. As other wrens, it is vociferous and more easily heard than seen. Preferring to remain within emergent marsh vegetation, it seldom offers unobscured views, but is often seen poking its head and chest out, or showing its backside just as it drops away into cover. The smaller, short-billed and straw-colored Sedge Wren is sometimes confused with this species, but is rare within the state.

Dark crown, white eye stripe, buffy upperparts, and blackish back with white stippling. Longish bill and expressive tail. Whitish underparts, often with buffy undertail.

Carolina Wren

Thryothorus ludovicianus

L 5" | **WS** 7"

Resident nearly throughout the state, the pleasing, melodious song of the rusty-colored Carolina Wren is one of our most routinely heard bird sounds. Offering considerable variation in their primary song, the most commonly heard song is often transcribed as "tea kettle, tea kettle, tea kettle, tea kettle." They may repeat other phrases instead, like "cheeseburger" or "troika," yet always maintain the churning, mechanical quality of their merry, energetic song. When excited, they cock their tail and emit scold calls, usually given from within dense understory. For as common and noisy as it is, this wren can be quite good at staying out of sight. Common in backyards, edge habitat, brushy thickets, and other understory habitats, it jumps about within bushes, shrubs, and tangled vegetation, seldom sitting out in plain view.

Ruddy brown above, buff-orange below with white throat, and long white eye stripe. Larger than other wrens.

Ruby-crowned Kinglet

Regulus calendula

L 4" | **WS** 6.75"

The curious, fidgety Ruby-crowned Kinglet bursts with attitude and energy and is as cute and charming a bird as there is. Often it seems overly bold for its tiny size, moving about at eye level or lower, seeming quite tame, and often revealing its scarlet crown patch. As it jostles amid shrubs, bushes and trees, it routinely shivers its wings, and utters curt call notes. The common call is a fast, two-noted *chit-chit* scold. A common migrant and winter visitor from September to May, it works hedgerows, thickets, forest edges, and treed parks in pursuit of small insects and spiders. Like its smaller cousin the Golden-crowned Kinglet, the Ruby-crowned hovers at the outer edges of branches when hunting, and joins mixed flocks of forest songbirds.

Small and olive-green overall with white eye ring and striking black-and-white wing bars. Watch for wing-flicking behavior.

Crown patch visible when excited. Short tail and thin bill.

Golden-crowned Kinglet

Regulus satrapa

L 3.75" | **WS** 6.25"

A tiny, round sprite that flits about restlessly in evergreen trees, the Golden-crowned Kinglet's bright yellow crown patch is distinctive. A common and widespread migrant and wintering species from October to April, it also breeds sparsely here within forests of the mountains and plateau. Breeding birds prefer tall coniferous trees such as spruces, hemlocks, or pines for nesting. Migrants are found in a variety of habitats, including smaller evergreen trees, bushes, brushy thickets, and mixed woodlots. It is most conspicuous in winter and as a migrant, and often occurs in pairs or small groups, readily joining mixed-species forest flocks, along with chickadees, wrens, and woodpeckers. Its common call is a rapid, very high-pitched set of rapid *see-see-see* notes.

Gold crest is most obvious when bird is agitated. Crown bordered on each side by black stripe, a white eye brow, and a dark "moustache."

Note dark patch in wing, pale face with dark eye.

Blue-gray Gnatcatcher

Polioptila caerulea

L 4" | **WS** 6.25"

Tiny, slender, and long-tailed, the well named Blue-gray Gnatcatcher is a conspicuous and spunky bird. Jumping and flitting
about the edges of mid- and upper stories of thickets, hedgerows,
semi-open woodlands, and woodlots, sometimes it joins mixed
species flocks with warblers, wrens, and chickadees. The common
call is an *eenh eenh* note, typically given a few notes at a time. A
common migrant and breeder statewide, it is present from April
through September. Its delicate cup-like nest is woven of spider
webs and placed on the top of a slender branch.

Gray overall, but males are
more bluish above and have
a dark eyebrow. White eye
ring. Long legs; long tail is
black with white sides.

Females grayer and less
blue than males. Bill is
slender and pointed.

Hermit Thrush

Catharus guttatus

L 6.25" | **WS** 10.5"

The Hermit Thrush is the only spotted brown thrush found here in winter. It prefers the understory of forest edges and brushy thickets, and sometimes hops around robin-like on lawns or roads near wooded cover. Migrants in spring and fall occur widely across the state, and it breeds in woodlands throughout much of the northern half of the state, and at higher elevations of the plateau and south along the mountains. The Hermit Thrush owns an ethereal song beginning with a long introductory whistle followed by a set of tinkling, rolling, twittering notes. Hermit Thrushes characteristically raise and lower their tail upon taking a perch, and when agitated flick and flex the wings and tail giving soft *chup* notes.

Reddish brown tail contrasts with grayer upperparts. Thin white eye ring.

Wood Thrush

Hylocichla mustelina

L 7.75" | **WS** 13"

One of our most accomplished songsters, the Wood Thrush's lovely song is a series of flute-like notes followed by liquid rattles. When agitated, it also gives a snappy *quip quip quip* call, but whether it is singing or calling, hearing the first Wood Thrush of the year is a sure sign that spring has arrived. Wintering in Central America, it occurs here from late April to October inhabiting shady mixed woodlots or moist deciduous forest. Hopping around on the ground, it works the shady forest floor, sticking its bill into leaf litter in search of spiders and insects. It perches in the mid- or lower story of the forest for singing, and forages on fruiting shrubs in the forest understory.

Largish thrush, plump and stout, with clear black spots on white underparts, and orange-brown above.

Veery
Catharus fuscescens

L 7" | **WS** 12"

A retiring forest thrush, the Veery is best known for its beautiful song. Thrushes generally are regarded as having some of the most beautiful bird vocalizations, and the Veery possesses a lovely burry, downward-spiraling song, perhaps similar to the sound a ball bearing would make while rolling down a drainpipe. Wintering in South America, it is a breeding bird present here from May through September. Migrants may turn up in thickets or in backyards that contain good cover and taller trees, but most often the Veery keeps to shady corners of humid woodlands, and so is usually easier to hear than to see. Feeding on the ground, it hops amid leaf litter in search of insects and also takes fruit from understory bushes and shrubs. It is found widely across the state, and good spots include Loyalsock State Forest, Forbes State Forest, and Wissahickon Valley Park.

Plain face lacks eye ring; indistinct orangish spotting on breast; evenly orangish brown above, head to tail.

Gray-cheeked Thrush

Catharus minimus

L 7.25" | **WS** 13"

Nesting in spruce forests in Canada, Alaska, and the Russian Far East and wintering in South America, this species occurs here only as a migrant in spring and autumn. Northbound birds are seen in mid- and late May, while southbound birds occur from mid-September to early October. The Gray-cheeked Thrush is shy and often hard to see, working within shady patches forest understory, but it occasionally visits backyards or forages in clearings near cover. Usually it is on or near the ground, where it hunts insects within the leaf litter, and takes fruit from the woodland understory. The Bicknell's Thrush is another thrush species that passes through Pennsylvania in the same period as Gray-cheeked, but occurs in smaller numbers and mostly in the east. It is identical in appearance to Gray-cheeked, but the two have slightly different vocalizations. Gray-cheeked's common *squeert* call is given in flight (especially when migrating at night) or from perches within the forest.

Plain gray face lacks warm tones and lacks an eye ring. Distinct black spotting on breast; olive-brown upperparts.

Swainson's Thrush
Catharus ustulatus

L 7" | **WS** 11.75"

The Swainson's Thrush is a common migrant throughout the state, and breeds sparsely. Most sightings are of migrants in May or from September to mid-October, when seen hopping along shady forest trails, woodland clearings, or edges of parks or yards near bushy cover or brush. The Swainson's nests in Pennsylvania mostly in hemlock forests in places like Ricketts Glen State Park, State Game Lands 13 and 57, Loyalsock State Forest, and Allegheny National Forest. Like the other thrushes in the genus *Catharus*, this bird is often more easily heard than seen, and spring migrants and breeding birds are often detected by voice. The song is a rising, burbling, string of phrases that spiral up the scale. It often is found near headwater streams and seeps where it flycatches more than the other spotted thrushes.

Bold eye ring and face are tinged with warm buff. Moderate spotting on breast; evenly olive-brown above from head to tail.

Eastern Bluebird

Sialia sialis

L 7" | **WS** 13"

A conspicuous thrush, the beautiful Eastern Bluebird is a common sight year-round along open country roads throughout most of the state. Preferring rural settings, fields and open spaces with scattered trees, posts, and wires for perching, bluebirds are often seen in pairs or small flocks. Foraging for insects and fruit, they flutter down to the ground and then return to exposed perches, and they are quite vocal. Calling especially when in flight, they give a soft, mellow *churr-bur*. They nest in tree cavities, old woodpecker holes, and readily adopt nest boxes. Males are bright blue above, while the females are grayer, and when the spotty gray juveniles emerge from the nest box and start taking up perches, they look so unlike the adults they are confusing to many birders.

Male bright blue above with bay-colored breast, white belly and white undertail.

Female grayish above with blue accents in wings and tail. Dingy brown breast and cheeks.

Juvenile has mottled spotted chest, pale spots on the back, with blue accents in the wings and tail.

American Robin

Turdus migratorius

L 9.5" | **WS** 14"

The American Robin, common at backyards, lawns, parks, woodland edges, and forests across the state, is among our best-known birds. A sturdy, strong-flying and handsome thrush, famous for hunting worms, the robin is a year-round resident, but the state hosts large numbers of migrants that breed farther north. It is a great nomad, and suddenly thousands may arrive to take advantage of fruiting trees. The robin is a conspicuous breeding bird, building messy, unkempt bowl-shaped nests of grass and mud, placed upon mid-story tree branches or under the eaves of houses. An active singer in even pre-dawn hours, it is one of the first birds to begin singing each day. The song typically consists of four to six short, clipped *cheery-up, clear-it* phrases. When alarmed, they give a shrill *Cleep! or Cleep! cleep! Clup-clup.*

Males are brick-red below with black head, mostly pale yellowish bill.

Females show less contrast. Grayer above, paler orangish below, with streaky throat.

Juveniles conspicuous and sometimes quite tame; underparts spotted.

Northern Mockingbird

Mimus polyglottos

L 10" | **WS** 14"

A celebrated songster, at home in urban parks, open suburban habitats with bushes and small trees, rural and agricultural settings, the mockingbird is one of our most familiar birds. Absent only from densely wooded areas of the high plateau and the mountains, the omnivorous mockingbird is a prolific singer, often observed sitting atop a wire, post, or other exposed perch singing away. Males learn and incorporate sounds from other bird species, and weave those into a song of their own. It is for this habit that it, along with its relatives the thrasher and catbird, are known as mimic thrushes. The mockingbird may sing inexhaustibly, even into the dead of night. The common call note is a loud, harsh *chick*. Highly territorial, it is a feisty bird given its slim appearance and light weight, and it is not unusual to see a mockingbird chasing other birds.

Long-tailed with pale gray plumage. White patches in wings and tail obvious in flight, but may be concealed at rest.

Mockingbirds guard their territory fiercely, chasing away and harassing intruders, including other birds (of all sizes), dogs, cats, and sometimes even people.

Juvenile has pale yellowish gape, and spots on underparts. Note all black eye; adults have dull orange iris.

Gray Catbird
Dumetella carolinensis

L 8.5" | **WS** 11"

The catbird is common and widespread throughout the state, skulking about amid dense cover, viny tangles, brushy thickets, and hedgerows. Typically seen on or close to the ground, despite its preference for keeping within cover, the catbird is a busybody, flopping and twitching within the vegetation, and usually revealing itself to an observer given some time. Common in backyards and edge habitat, it is named for its catlike mewing call, but also owns a complex song, a jumbled assortment of chirps, squeals, and chatters, sounds borrowed from other birds' vocal repertoire. It is scarce in winter, with most sightings in the southeast, but catbirds storm back in spring and are abundant here from April to October.

Long-tailed, an even gray overall, with black crown. Slender, strong black bill good for eating fruit and taking insects.

Smallest of the mimic thrushes, with chestnut-brown undertail, and dark eye.

Brown Thrasher

Toxostoma rufum

L 11.5" | **WS** 13"

A large mimic thrush, the Brown Thrasher sneaks around amid dense cover, stalking the shady ground beneath hedgerows or thickets in search of bugs, seeds, or fruit. It perches in plain view occasionally when singing. It possesses one of the most extensive ranges of sounds of any bird, and its song incorporates elements from many other bird species, with phrases typically doubled. Common call notes include a smacking *tsick!* and a hoarse, throaty *hurr* or *henh;* the latter is often given at dawn. A common breeding bird across most of the state from April to October, it is scarce or rare in winter, usually in the southeast.

Long tail and long bill, red-brown above, with dark streaks below. Yellow eyes. Skulking behavior.

European Starling

Sturnus vulgaris

L 8.5" | **WS** 14"

The pudgy starling is routinely encountered across the state, from city centers to suburban and rural settings. Common around human habitations, they avoid woodlands, but are otherwise widespread and abundant. Usually in flocks, they feed on grassy lawns, or in fields, sometimes with cowbirds and blackbirds. Sometimes starlings gather in large evening roosts, making quite a racket. Common calls include a muttered *prrurt*, often given in flight. Starlings skillfully imitate sounds of many other birds, including Northern Bobwhite, Eastern Wood-Pewee, and Killdeer. Starlings nest in tree cavities, woodpecker holes, and nest boxes. Introduced from Eurasia, they compete aggressively with native cavity-nesting birds for nest sites. They easily displace bluebirds, woodpeckers, and even kestrels; consequently, they are often regarded as a nuisance.

Nonbreeding adults are finely patterned, with pale spots and stipples. Bill is mostly dark.

Breeding adults are beautiful glossy purplish with yellow bill.

Cedar Waxwing
Bombycilla cedrorum

L 6" | **WS** 10.25"

Striking and attractive, the dapper Cedar Waxwing is a nomadic, fruit-eating bird, at home in a variety of treed habitats. From urban parks to suburban settings, golf courses, hedgerows, and woodland edges, waxwings move about restlessly in tight flocks with a buzzy flight. Present year-round, they breed across the state, but due to a diet that is mostly fruit (although they fly-catch on occasion) they begin nesting later than most other songbirds. Waxwing nests are sometimes parasitized by cowbirds, but cowbird chicks cannot sustain such a fruit-heavy diet and usually fail to fledge. The waxwing has a limited vocal repertoire, offering extremely high-pitched *sseeeeeeeeee* sounds, which have a ringing quality at close range.

Adult caramel-brown with a black mask and crest, and yellowish belly. Yellow tail band and waxy red tips to wings. Juvenile mottled and streaky gray.

American Pipit

Anthus rubescens

L 6" | **WS** 10.5"

Slender with a long tail and fine bill, the pipit is a bird of open country and barren landscapes, such as dirt fields or fields with short grass, turf farms, beaches, exposed shorelines and flats. Present only as migrants and winter visitors from October to April, pipits occur both singly and in flocks. They frequently call in flight, issuing a rapid-fire, high-pitched *tzi-tzi-tzi-tzi*. On the ground, they walk with a steady pace, and when they pause, they pump their tail up and down, unlike other field birds. Pipits are nomadic and somewhat unpredictable, but look for them at Yellow Creek State Park, along Mud Level Road in Cumberland County, or at Struble Lake.

Nonbreeding birds are olive-gray above and creamy below with gray streaking. Pale buffy moustachial stripe and faint eye line.

Snow Bunting
Plectrophenax nivalis

L 10" | **WS** 11"

An Arctic breeder, this attractive cold-weather bird of open
country, barren ground, stubble fields, beaches, and shorelines
occurs unpredictably in the state. Nearly all Snow Buntings in our
area are found from November into March, and their numbers vary
from year to year. Search at the Imperial Grasslands, around
Curllsville (Clarion County), along Mud Level Road (Cumberland
County), near Limestoneville and Turbotville, and in the fields
south of Kutztown. Typically, Snow Buntings flock in numbers
from a just a few to several hundred individuals. They are strong-
flying and nomadic, showing boldly patterned black-and-white
wings in flight. They vocalize frequently, and common calls
include a strong, rapid, rattled *chit-titta-tik* often followed by a
sweet *teeyoo*.

Adults in winter are a
combination of rust,
white, and black, with
striking wing pattern.
Males are whiter than
females. In flight, note
bold wing pattern,
notched tail.

Yellow-breasted Chat

Icteria virens

L 7" | **WS** 9.75"

The fascinating Yellow-breasted Chat is gorgeous and secretive. It inhabits thickets, hedgerows, shrubby areas along waterways, and scrubby overgrown fields. Chats bedevil birders with a strange array of sounds as they hide deep in cover tantalizing those who wish to see them. The typical song is reminiscent of a mimic thrush, with short phrases, sometimes repeated, but the phrases are delivered more deliberately. Often it is easiest to see a chat is when it is singing, and at times they take semi-exposed perches. On nesting territories they flutter up to sing in dramatic aerial displays, sometimes in the moonlight. Most chats are observed in the southern half of the state from May to July, when they are vocal and easy to detect. Southbound migrants continue into October, but given their secretive habits, they are harder to find once they have gone quiet for the fall.

Bright yellow below; unmarked olive above; black lores are bordered by white stripes.

Ovenbird
Seiurus aurocapilla

L 6" | **WS** 9.5"

Walking on the forest floor the streak-chested, Ovenbird strides
along with a spasmodic, bouncy gait as it searches for bugs
within leaf litter. Named for its dome-shaped nest, built on the
ground with the opening on the side, it is a unique terrestrial
warbler at home in a variety of mixed and deciduous woodlands. In its appearance and habits, it recalls a small *Catharus*
thrush. Its larger size than most other warblers contributes to
that impression. The song of the Ovenbird resonates at woodlands across the state starting with their arrival in April. When
perched amid the lower or mid-story of the forest, it belts out a
loud *tea-cher, tea-cher, tea-cher, tea-cher*. It breeds throughout
Pennsylvania, but winters to our south and vanishes by early
October. Once in a while, one remains into the winter. Migrants
in spring and fall occur even in highly urban settings, so long as
there is a shady bush to hide under.

Olive-brown above with
black streaks on breast,
white belly. White eye
ring, black head stripes;
orange on crown is
sometimes hard to see.

Louisiana Waterthrush

Parkesia motacilla

L 6" | **WS** 10"

Find yourself a babbling brook, or a meandering wooded creek
and you have a chance to see this sturdy, sweet-singing, riparian
warbler. It is associated with cold streams in forested areas,
arriving during the first days of trout season. Good spots to
search in spring or summer include Powdermill Run, the Juniata
River, the Delaware Water Gap, or Wissahickon Valley Park.
Keeping to shaded stream-sides, this waterthrush walks the edge
of the water, hunting insects in muddy areas or leaf litter, and
bobbing up and down as it goes. Wintering in the Neotropics, it
one of the earliest spring migrants to return to breed, sometimes
back in southern Pennsylvania by late March. It departs early in
fall, often gone by the end of August. The two waterthrushes are
difficult to distinguish, but differ in structure, habits, plumage
details, and voice. An impressive songster, the Louisiana's song
begins with beautiful long, down-slurred, fluid notes and ends in
a jumbled series of short, choppy notes.

Stocky thrush-like warbler with long
pinkish legs. Similar to Northern
Waterthrush, but heavier, larger bill,
bolder eye stripe, little streaking on
throat, and streaking on underparts
is blurrier. Often shows smudgy, buffy
wash at the rear flanks.

Northern Waterthrush

Parkesia noveboracensis

L 6" | **WS** 9.5"

At home in bogs, swampy areas, and dank, dark pockets in wooded areas or thickets, the Northern Waterthrush is a common migrant in spring and fall. Wintering in the Neotropics, it occurs in Pennsylvania from May to September, breeding at scattered sites in the northern half of the state and south along the Alleghenies. Preferring wooded wetlands or thickets near slow-moving creeks or patches of still water, it nests at higher elevations and farther upstream than the Louisiana Waterthrush. Though the two overlap on occasion, generally the Northern prefers flatter, less hilly areas. A shy bird, it forages on the ground for insects, and as it walks it bobs its tail up and down, calling often. The common call note is a loud, resonant *Tsink!* The song is a set of cheerful, choppy notes, "see-it see-it see-it so, what-what-how."

Olive-brown above, and streaky below with pale eyebrow. Averages smaller than Louisiana, has a narrower eyebrow, with smaller bill, often yellowish-tinged underparts, and darker legs. Small streaks extend onto the throat.

Worm-eating Warbler

Helmitheros vermivorum

L 4.5–5.25" | **WS** 9"

Jaunty and trim, the Worm-eating Warbler is a lively little bird, keeping to dimly lit patches of forest. Foraging low to the ground in sloping woodlands with dense understory including rhododendron and viburnum, it hunts amid clusters of dry or dead leaves in search of caterpillars. Though it feeds and nests low in the forest, it ventures up to mid-story perches to sing its dry, insect-like song, which is a buzzy trill similar to the song of Chipping Sparrow but usually faster, shorter, and flatter. Present as a migrant and breeder from May into September. Migrants occur widely, but breeding birds are mostly in the mountains or the Piedmont. Search for it along the Kittatinny Ridge, the Frankstown Branch of the Juniata River, the Allegheny River in Clarion County, and at Tuscarora State Forest.

Striking head pattern with black stripes breaking up ochre head, face, and throat. Olive upperparts.

Black-and-white Warbler

Mniotilta varia

L 5.25" | **WS** 8.25"

This zebra-striped, tree-creeping warbler is distinctive in plumage and behavior. Crawling along and around on tree trunks and branches, searching for insects within cracks and crevices of bark, this charming little bird acts more like a nuthatch than a warbler. Foraging at all levels within the forest, it usually chooses a mid-story perch for singing, and it churns out a very high-pitched, ringing set of notes, commonly described as sounding like a squeaky wagon wheel. Present from April to mid-October, the Black-and-white Warbler is a common migrant and breeding bird, found in an array of woodland habitats, with breeding birds preferring mixed or deciduous forests. It is widespread across the state, but good areas to see it on its breeding grounds are Loyalsock State Forest and the north-central forests and state game lands.

Distinctive black-and-white striped plumage with nuthatch-like behavior. Male (pictured) has black on throat and cheeks. Females white below with white throat, less contrasting markings on undertail compared to male.

Blue-winged Warbler

Vermivora cyanoptera

L 4.75" | **WS** 7.5"

This dazzling little warbler is an early migrant, arriving in late April, and many stay here to breed in shrubby hedgerows, overgrown thickets, and bushy swamps in much of the state. On breeding territories and in spring migration, males sing a high-pitched buzzy *tseeee-bizzzzzzzzz* song. Like most other warblers, the Blue-winged stops singing in late summer, and by the end of September they have all left the state, headed for their Neotropical wintering grounds. The Blue-winged is closely related to the Golden-winged Warbler, and the two species interbreed, producing hybrids known as "Brewster's" Warblers, "Lawrence's" Warblers, and other hybrids that do not fit neatly into either category.

Male golden yellow with gray-blue wings and white wing bars, undertail, and outer tail. Black bill and eye line.

Female similar to male but drabber, less richly colored.

Golden-winged Warbler

Vermivora chrysoptera

L 4.75" | **WS** 7.5"

A clean-cut, stately warbler, the Golden-winged is found in semi-open secondary-growth tangles and brush, along power line cuts, regenerating clear cuts, blowdown areas, moist thickets, and swampy shrublands near mature deciduous forest. This is a scarce breeding bird and rarely detected as a migrant. Most are seen in May and June in the Allegheny and Pocono mountains or at sites within the ridges and valleys. During these months adults sound off, singing with a trill followed by several shorter buzzing notes. Fall migrants in August and September are harder to find. Search for this bird at Bald Eagle State Park, Sproul State Forest, the Scotia Barrens, and Delaware State Forest. Golden-winged hybridizes with the Blue-winged, and hybrids have intermediate plumages and sing either song or both species' songs.

Males have chickadee-like head pattern, with yellow crown and wing bar.

Female is similar but drabber, less clean-cut.

Prothonotary Warbler

Protonotaria citrea

L 5.5" | **WS** 8.75"

The stout Prothonotary Warbler makes for some serious eye candy. Wintering in the Neotropics, it is a scarce migrant and local breeder, and most sightings are in May or June. After that, the Prothonotary becomes quieter and harder to find, but occasionally a migrant is seen in August or September. A bird of wet woods and swamps, search for it along the lower Susquehanna River such as at the Conejohela Flats, or at Conneaut-Geneva Marsh or Peace Valley Park. Like most warblers, the best way to find the Prothonotary is to listen for its song, a loud, ringing series of *reet reet reet reet reet* notes.

Brilliant yellow with blue-gray wings and green back. Large black eye and bill. White undertail contrasts with yellow belly.

Females similar to males but dingier. When it takes flight, note white within tail feathers.

Yellow Warbler

Setophaga petechia

L 5" | **WS** 7"

Aptly named, the Yellow Warbler is entirely yellow and owns a sweet melodic song. Its characteristic "sweet sweet so so sweet" song rings out from creekside willows, moist shrublands, and wet brushy areas, across the state in spring and summer. Wintering in Central and South America, this is one of our most common songbirds from April to October. It is a confiding bird, often offering observers good views as it works within the outer branches and twigs of smaller trees and bushy shrubs, hopping about in search of caterpillars and insects. Some females and especially first-autumn Yellow Warblers can be drab yellow-olive or even grayish. These can be confused with female Wilson's Warblers or female Common Yellowthroats, but note Yellow's uniform appearance, pale face, and pale edges on the rear, inner wing (tertials).

Males are bright yellow with chestnut streaks on the breast.

Females are more muted yellow, but similar in shape. Crisp pale tertial edges and yellow-green tail.

Tennessee Warbler

Oreothlypis peregrina

L 4.75" | **WS** 7.75"

Small and slight with a short, sharp bill, the Tennessee Warbler passes through the Keystone State only in migration. Breeding in boreal forests to our north and wintering in the Neotropics, it shows up here in May and reappears when southbound in late August to early October. Usually observed at the mid-story or upper story of woodlands and woodlots, it is occasionally lower in brushy thickets. A relatively nondescript warbler that is somewhat vireo-like in appearance, the Tennessee uses its fine, pointed bill to obtain nectar from plants while on the wintering grounds, but on the breeding grounds it specializes on spruce budworms. Its abundance, like that of the Cape May and Bay-breasted Warblers, is tied to fluctuations in the northern budworm populations. Search for it at Presque Isle State Park, at Frick Park in Pittsburgh, or at Heinz National Wildlife Refuge.

Gray head with green back, white underparts. Head with pale eyebrow and dark line through the eye.

Females have similar eyebrow and eye line, but are duller. Pale white or whitish undertail help distinguish Tennessee from similar Orange-crowned. First-fall females can be yellowish overall.

Orange-crowned Warbler

Oreothlypis celata

L 5" | **WS** 7.5"

The Orange-crowned Warbler is generally scarce from September to May. Its migration peaks in mid-September to mid-October, and while it is not reliably found anywhere, it is worth watching for at Presque Isle, and at other good fall birding spots, such as Pennypack on the Delaware. Typically it is found near the ground, actively flitting about in open areas with larger bushes, weedy fields, thickets, or keeping to the understory at woodland edges. Its call note is useful for identification as it offers up a crisp, clear chip note while foraging.

Uniform green, with pale yellowish eye ring, and yellow-green undertail. Overall color varies from gray-green to yellow-green. Almost never shows any orange on crown.

Nashville Warbler

Oreothlypis ruficapilla

L 4.25" | **WS** 7.25"

A dapper, active little warbler, the Nashville occurs here mostly as a northbound migrant in May or when southbound in September and October, but it also breeds sparingly in the northern half of the state and at a few sites in the mountains. Preferring treed hedgerows, thickets, brushy woodlands, bogs, and forest edge, migrant Nashvilles flit and hop, jumping between thin outer branches of small to medium-size trees, while searching for insects. Spring migrants and breeding birds are often most easily found by listening for their melodic song, a series of five or six *tut-sit* phrases strung together and followed by a fluid trill. The Nashville is a common migrant, but to see it on its breeding grounds search at Loyalsock State Forest, State Game Lands 13 and 57, or in boggy areas of the Pocono Mountains.

Gray head with yellow throat and underparts, bold white eye ring. Finely pointed bill. Green back; often whitish or pale at the legs.

Females and first-autumn birds are more uniform olive gray. Yellow-green undertail; white eye ring; whitish at legs.

Mourning Warbler
Geothlypis philadelphia

L 4 - 6 " | **WS** 7 "

Keeping low to the ground in dense understory of woodlands and brushy thickets, the Mourning Warbler is tough to see. Named "mourning" for the male's funereal hood, this species is an uncommon migrant and a scarce breeding bird. Nesting in the northern part of the state, especially between Crawford and Potter counties, it prefers regenerating woodlands with dense stands of small trees, shrubs and blackberry bushes near taller stands. A late migrant in spring often not seen until the second half of May, it departs early in fall, passing through in August before disappearing in September. Its skulking habits, scarcity, beautiful plumage pattern and pleasing shape, make it a sought-after bird. Search for it in the Allegheny National Forest and Loyalsock State Forest in May and June when males are singing. The song is a pleasing, warbling *cheery, cheery, cheery, churry churr,* a song often heard in radio and television commercials.

Males have gray head with black bib, yellow underparts, and green upperparts. Heavy bill.

Female less crisply marked than male. First-fall birds confused with female Common Yellowthoat but heavier, with yellower belly, and pale eye arcs.

Kentucky Warbler
Geothlypis formosa

L 5.25" | **WS** 8.5"

Smartly attired, the Kentucky is a hefty warbler, staying low within wet woodlands. Feeding on or near the ground on insects, migrants are reclusive and hard to see. Search for it in Sewickley Heights Borough Park near Pittsburgh and in appropriate habitat in Westmoreland and Fayette counties. The Kentucky needs sizable chunks of deciduous forest for breeding, and is often found near creeks or drainages. It nests fairly commonly in the southwest and spottily elsewhere in the south, including the lower Susquehanna area. Wintering in the Neotropics, it breeds here from May to July, and on territory sings a melodious *cheery, cheery, cheery, cheery, cheery* sometimes sounding similar to a Carolina Wren.

Bold yellow eyebrow, black cheeks, yellow underparts, and green back and tail. Black crown often shows bits of gray. Looks leggy compared to Common Yellowthroat, which lacks yellow eyebrow.

Common Yellowthroat

Geothlypis trichas

L 4.75" | **WS** 6.75"

Small and sprightly, this aptly named warbler is common in
Pennsylvania and its yellow throat is one of its most noticeable
features. Frequenting marshes, moist meadows, overgrown fields,
and thickets throughout the state, it is rare in winter, but is
widespread from April to October. Its measured, musical song is a
routine sound of spring and summer. The common song is a series
of *witch-adee, witch-adee, witch-adee* phrases and the call note,
heard often, is a harsh, lip-smacking *tetch* or *tchep*. Staying low
in rank or brushy vegetation, yellow throats behave somewhat
similarly to a small wren, cocking up their tail, and flitting short
distances between dense patches of cover.

Male with black mask and rich
yellow throat is distinctive.

Females and first-fall
yellowthroats are drab olive,
but the yellow throat
contrasts with olive green
cheeks and upperparts. Eye
ring is not bold; no eyebrow.

Hooded Warbler

Setophaga citrina

L 5.25" | **WS** 7"

A startlingly gorgeous bird of the forest understory, the Hooded Warbler is one flashy bird. Keeping to the depths of the undergrowth of deciduous woodlands or mixed woodlots, it offers glimmers of yellow through the vegetation, flashing its white tail feathers as it flits. It can be hard to see well, but fortunately for us, this treasure of a bird is a fairly common breeder. Heading south for the Neotropics in September, Hoodeds return here in May as migrants and at breeding sites. Nesting throughout most of the west and eastward along mountains/valleys, look for it at sites such as Allegheny National Forest, Powdermill Nature Reserve, Forbes State Forest, and Michaux State Forest. It is most easily found by listening for its song, a sweet *tu-wee, tu-wee, tu-weety-oo,* somewhat similar to the Magnolia Warbler's song, but louder and more forceful.

Striking black hood, yellow mask, yellow underparts, green back with white in outer tail.

Females show contrast between yellow face and olive crown. Some lack black on head, others have partial hood. Look for white in the outer tail as it moves.

Wilson's Warbler

Cardellina pusilla

L 4.25" | **WS** 6"

One of five species named for the famed Philadelphia ornithologist Alexander Wilson (1766-1813), the Wilson's Warbler stays near to the ground, preferring thickets and woodlands with a good scrubby understory. It occurs only as a migrant, northbound in May when heading for the breeding grounds around boreal forest bogs and lakes. Spring migrants may sing, issuing a set of choppy, sputtered chip notes, *tsip tsip tsup tsup tsert tsert tsert*. At the close of the breeding season, they pass through in September, heading for Central America for the winter.

Small and slim, with slender tail and short bill. Male has neat black cap.

Female lacks black in crown but like male, has big dark eye, yellow eyebrow, and rich yellow underparts and greenish upperparts. Tail is yellow-green.

American Redstart

Setophaga ruticilla

L 5.25" | **WS** 7.75"

The slender, little redstart is a charmer as it spins and dashes with quick movements, fanning its tail to flash its characteristic tail pattern. From May into September, this attractively marked warbler is a common migrant and breeder, nesting in much of the state's woodlands. Redstarts hunt small insects usually in the mid-story or upper story of the forest canopy, and they give voice often. Their song is remarkably variable, but one song type heard regularly is a *spree spree sree sris*. Songs generally involve a couple to a dozen high-pitched phrases strung together, and both sexes offer a snappy, high, thin *tsic* call note.

Immature male with yellow on side of breast and black "freckles" on face.

Female gray with yellow on wings, tail, and sides of breast.

Adult male black and orange, including tail; white belly.

Northern Parula

Setophaga americana

L 4.5" | **WS** 7"

A tiny, short-tailed warbler, the Northern Parula is a woodland gem. Spry and dapper, it flits about the mid- and upper story, hunting for insects and singing its buzzy song, a rising *zreee zreee zreee, ziz ziz z zee*. The song is variable, and some sounds similar to Black-throated Blue Warbler or Cerulean Warbler. Absent in winter, they return in late April and are common migrants in spring and fall, occupying brushy thickets, treed parks, woodlots, and forests. It is one of the most widespread breeding warblers in the state. Famous for using lichens and moss to construct their nests, they prefer woods with wet areas or creeks and tall trees, including some conifers. By late August, they are headed south for Central America and the Caribbean, and then are found in places where songbirds gather such as Presque Isle, Heinz National Wildlife Refuge, and Pittsburgh's Frick Park.

Blue-gray head, black lores, white eye arcs, yellow chest, white belly. Male has black and reddish collar.

Yellow throat contrasts with white belly; white wing bars; green back patch. Female has paler face, drabber blue-gray above.

The Northern Parula's song is a variable series of buzzy chirps, ascending in speed and pitch.

Cape May Warbler

Setophaga tigrina

L 4.75" | **WS** 8.25"

Breeding in boreal forests and wintering in the West Indies, the
Cape May Warbler passes through only as a migrant. Spring
migrants occur in May but are scarce. Southbound fall migrants
are more numerous, yet still fairly uncommon, from August into
October. They forage in coniferous woodland canopy for insects in
the outer branches. The Cape May is also seen nectaring at
flowering plants, but when nesting it specializes on spruce
budworms. Its abundance each year is tied to that insect's abundance. Named by Alexander Wilson for the epic bird migration site
in southern New Jersey, this warbler's plumage varies consider-
ably. Spring males are richly colored, but young in their first fall
(especially females) are dull olive with only faint streaking below.

Male has yellow
face and
underparts, with
black streaking
below. Cheeks are
chestnut; prominent
white wing bar.
Sharp bill is black.

Female gray-green, with
more subdued streaking
below. Some lack yellow
tones and wing bars, but
pale sides of the neck
contrast with darker nape.
Rump pale green or
yellow-green.

Cerulean Warbler

Setophaga cerulea

L 4.75" | **WS** 7.75"

Good views of this stunning azure woodland warbler are rare,
making the Cerulean Warbler one of the most sought-after birds.
They keep to the treetops and even at known breeding sites, they
nest within expanses of deciduous woodlands, making them hard
to pinpoint. The best way to locate one is by the song, a buzzy
series of high-pitched phrases, *zree zree zree, zurra zurra zeeeeeee*.
Search for them at the Frankstown Branch of the Juniata River
and along the Delaware Water Gap during May and June. This
sublime sprite has undergone a steep decline in recent decades.
Degradation of its wintering habitat in South America, combined
with fragmentation of forests here, have hurt the bird's population
badly, and it is now a species of high concern in the state.

Brilliant blue above, but more often seen from below; note the clean white underparts, dark collar, streaks on flanks.

Adult females are aqua, with wing bars, a faint collar, and streaks down the flanks. First-fall females are greener above; the pale underparts are tinged yellow.

Black-throated Blue Warbler

Setophaga caerulescens

L 5.25" | **WS** 7.75"

The male Black-throated Blue is a handsome warbler. Wintering in the Neotropics, it makes its way north in the spring, arriving here in late April, when its rising, slurring, burry *zwurr zwurr zweeee* song is heard commonly in woodlands. Migrants are found in forests, woodlots, parks and yards with tall trees, and brushy thickets. Breeding birds require larger expanses of deciduous or mixed woods with good understory, such as rhododendron. Keeping fairly low when foraging, it may take a higher perch to sing. To see the Black-throated Blue where it nests, search at the Allegheny National Forest, Tiadaghton State Forest, or Ricketts Glen State Park. In late August, heading south, they are seen commonly into mid-October.

Male is well named, with blue back and tail, black face and flanks, and bright white on the belly. Distinctive white wing patch.

Females are very different, being olive overall with a pale eyebrow, pale eye crescent, and paler moustachial stripe. Most have white wing patch like male, but some females lack this.

Blackburnian Warbler

Setophaga fusca

L 5" | **WS** 8.5"

Bursting with sherbet orange, the adult male Blackburnian Warbler is stunningly beautiful, and a quality sighting leaves you speechless. Named for the famous English naturalist Anna Blackburne, this is a bird at home in the treetops of various woodland types. Spring migrants and breeders, like other warblers, are often best found by listening for their song which is lengthy and high-pitched, ascending to almost inaudibly high frequency at the end. Breeding in cool forests on the high plateau, mostly in the northern half of Pennsylvania, search for it in places like Hearts Content in Allegheny National Forest and Ricketts Glen State Park, and this warbler is also seen widely during migration in May and September.

Male stunning sherbet-orange on head and chest, with largely black upperparts and large white wing patch.

Female less orange; sometimes the face shows only a suffusion of pale yellow. Like male, it has dark cheek, wing bars, faint streaks on flanks.

Chestnut-sided Warbler

Setophaga pensylvanica

L 5" | **WS** 7.75"

The dapper Chestnut-sided Warbler moves about with its tail cocked up, preferring semi-open forest and tree gap areas with good understory, especially with mountain laurel. It is a common migrant and a regular breeding bird, and the only breeding species whose scientific name commemorates our state. Wintering in the Neotropics, the Chestnut-sided is found here from late April into October. It breeds commonly in game lands and forests across the northern half of the state, and south along the Allegheny Mountains. Look for it in the Allegheny National Forest or at Ricketts Glen State Park. Listen for the song, a fast, ringing "please please pleased to meet ya."

Adults white below, with black streaked back, chestnut flanks, black moustache and eye line, and yellow crown.

In autumn, nonbreeding birds have green upperparts, white eye ring, pale gray underparts, yellowish wing bars.

Bay-breasted Warbler

Setophaga castanea

L 5.5" | **WS** 9"

Wintering in the Caribbean and in northern South America, and breeding in spruce forests across Canada and New England, the Bay-breasted Warbler graces Pennsylvania only during migration. They pass through in May, keeping to the treetops, making them harder to see, and they prefer woodlands with conifers. Their high-pitched song can be hard to pick out amid the din of louder songbirds, and it somewhat recalls the squeaky wagon-wheel song of the Black-and-white Warbler, but Bay-breasted's is a *teetzee teetzee teetzee* or a faster *tzee tzee tzee tzee*. Fall migrants move south through the state mostly in September, and appear very different than in spring but similar to fall Blackpoll Warblers, being greenish above but with an unstreaked chest and a buff wash to the pale undertail. Bay-breasted Warbler numbers vary from year to year depending on availability of spruce budworms, the species' primary source of food on their breeding grounds.

Breeding male has bay crown, throat, and flanks. Cream-buff neck-patch. Black face and streaky back.

Breeding female grayish, with hints of bay on crown and throat, white wing bars.

Blackpoll Warbler
Setophaga striata

L 5.5" | **WS** 9"

Migrating north in May and southbound in September and October, this species breeds in the boreal forest of Canada and Alaska and winters in South America. Migrants in Pennsylvania are found in a variety of woodland habitats, often near water, but they also turn up in brushy thickets. Spring birds seem to arrive all at once, a little later than most other warblers in mid-May, and they sing frequently. The song varies, but is often a rapid series of extremely high-pitched notes, a persistent *tsst tsst tsst tsst tss ss* that trails off, somewhat resembling the sound some cars make when in need of brake fluid. In autumn they are similar to the Bay-breasted Warbler.

Adult male in spring has black crown, white cheeks, and black moustache, streaked breast and sides. Yellowish legs. Compare with fall Black-and-white Warbler.

Female pale grayish, sometimes tinged yellow or green. Streaky overall with wing bars.

Fall birds are greenish with white undertail, and faint streaks on breast. Legs or feet usually pale. Fairly prominent dark eye line. Compare with Bay-breasted Warbler.

Palm Warbler

Setophaga palmarum

L 5.5" | **WS** 8"

The conspicuous, tail-pumping Palm Warbler is more terrestrial in its habits than most other warblers and is more at home in open or semi-open habitats. Poorly named, the Palm Warbler breeds in the boreal forest to our north, and though many winter around the Caribbean and the Gulf of Mexico, they seldom use palm trees. Usually they forage on or near the ground for small insects or seed, in edge habitats, fields, lawns, and thickets. Migrants head north in April and May and are southbound in September and October. Often a very few spend the winter in the state's southeast. Two subspecies occur, the more colorful "Yellow" and the browner "Western" Palm Warbler.

Sexes are similar. Palm is a rather flat-crowned, long-tailed, with an olive-colored rump. "Western" (pictured here) is browner, with yellow-olive rump and undertail. Breeding birds have rich brown crown.

"Yellow" Palm is wholly yellow below, and warmer brown above than "Western." Both show small white spots in outer tail, most noticeable in flight.

Pine Warbler

Setophaga pinus

L 5.5" | **WS** 8.75"

The long-tailed Pine Warbler varies tremendously in plumage color between bright adult males and drab females. As the name suggests, they are strongly tied to areas with pine trees and usually keep to the upper branches of pines. They are quite vocal, giving a rich warbling, trilling song, similar to the drier song of the Chipping Sparrow. Unlike most other warblers, the Pine winters almost entirely in the southeastern United States. It is rare in southeastern Pennsylvania in winter, and is mostly seen from late March to October. Good spots to look for it include Yellow Creek State Park, Sproul State Forest, and Beltzville State Park.

Males are yellow on throat and chest, with white wing bars, blackish lores, and a green back, head, and cheeks.

Female is less yellow, often dull brown overall with white wing bars.

Yellow-rumped Warbler

Setophaga coronata

L 5" | **WS** 8.25"

A conspicuous little songbird, common in a variety of woodland, shrubland or thicket habitats, the Yellow-rumped Warbler sallies out from foliage to nab insects, or moves nimbly within vegetation as it forages for fruit. The yellow rump patch is easily seen as it flits about, but is sometimes concealed by the wing tips when the bird is at rest. Heartier than most other warblers, some Yellow-rumpeds are able to overwinter here, but most are seen as abundant migrants in April and May and especially when southbound in October. It is a fairly common breeding bird in the northern half of Pennsylvania, nesting in coniferous forest or mixed woodlands with scattered evergreens. In summer it breeds at Ricketts Glen State Park and Loyalsock State Forest, and in winter it is often seen at Presque Isle.

Male has black mask, white throat, bluish upperparts, and black streaking on breast and flanks. Breeding female similar but less strikingly patterned.

Yellow-throated Warbler

Setophaga dominica

L 5.5" | **WS** 8"

An elegant warbler, the Yellow-throated is found in tall trees along waterways, where it gives a long, sweet, descending song that rises slightly at the end: *see see see-ert see-ert see-ert, so so sweet.* Absent in winter, it is an early migrant returning often in mid-April. It prefers to nest in sycamores or sometimes pines, and at times creeps along tree branches resembling a nuthatch. Look for it along the rivers south of the Pittsburgh, along the Frankstown Branch of the Juniata River, and along the lower Susquehanna River. After they stop singing in July, they become much harder to find, and migrants are seldom detected as they move south in August and September.

Long heavy bill and long tail. Yellow confined to throat and upper breast. White eyebrow contrasts with black eye line, and black cheek extends down the chest onto the flanks as streaking. White belly and white wing bars.

Prairie Warbler

Setophaga discolor

L 4.75" | **WS** 7"

Keeping to scrubby meadows, thickets, woodland gaps, and power line cuts, this warbler is less a bird of the prairie than of regenerating forest areas. The Prairie Warbler is found here during migration and as a breeding bird. Returning from wintering grounds in Florida and the Caribbean in April, it nests at scattered sites across the state, often where there are young pine or cedar trees but also in small deciduous trees. Look for them in the Imperial Grasslands, the Curllsville Strips, Ricketts Glen State Park, or the State Game Lands in Berks County. Listen for their song, which rises in a series of rapid, thin, burry whistled *swee, swee, swee, swee, szee, zee, zee, zi, zi, zsss* notes. They cease singing in July and begin dispersing south in August, with stragglers remaining through September.

Adults yellow below, green above, with black eye line, "bridle," and streaks down the flanks. Often pumps the tail.

Black-throated Green Warbler

Setophaga virens

L 5.25" | **WS** 7.75"

From late April to July, as a spring migrant and breeding bird,
the Black-throated Green's sing-song *see see see su-zy* or *zoo
zee, zoo-zoo zee* is one of the easiest warbler songs to recognize.
Like most migrant songbirds, it ceases to sing in July, but is
encountered as a migrant into October. Breeding in coniferous or
mixed woodlands throughout the northern half of the state, and
south along the mountains, it is often associated with hemlock
forest, but it nests also in deciduous woodlands to a lesser
extent. Migrants appear in woodlots and thickets, but very often
the Black-throated Green keeps to the upper edge of the forest,
providing views mostly of its belly. In these situations, keep an
eye out for the yellowish band between the legs and the white
undertail coverts, a useful field mark.

Male has yellow face, black
throat, breast, and flank streaks.
Note white wing bars, and faint
yellow-green wash by the legs.

Female smudged black on
sides of neck and breast.
Yellow face with greenish
cheeks, white wing bars, and
yellow-green wash at legs.

Magnolia Warbler

Setophaga magnolia

L 5" | **WS** 7.5"

More a bird of coniferous woodlands than magnolia trees, this warbler nests mostly in spruces and hemlocks, but away from breeding areas it is found in a variety of woodland and thicket habitats. A common and widespread migrant in May and September, the Magnolia breeds in the northern half of the state and in parts of the mountains. Look for it in the Allegheny National Forest, Loyalsock State Forest, and Ricketts Glen State Park, and listen for its short, whistled *teetsoo whee teetsoo whee teetsoo* song.

Male is yellow below with black back, collar, and blurry streaks down the breast. White eyebrow, eye crescent, and wing bars; yellow rump.

First-year female is gray and yellow, with gray collar, and greenish back. White undertail coverts, wing bars. When seen from below note the distinctive undertail pattern, with basal half white and outer half black.

Canada Warbler
Cardellina canadensis

L 4-6" | **WS** 6.75-8.75"

A songbird of dense forest understory seemingly always on the move, the Canada Warbler can be tough to see as it keeps to the dark corners of the forest. Most of this dapper warbler's population breeds in Canada, but this species also nests in Pennsylvania. Present here from May to September, it winters in the Neotropics and is a late migrant, returning here from mid-May into early June. It nests at scattered sites in the northern half of the state and south along the mountains, usually in coniferous or mixed woodlands. Southbound migrants depart early, but stragglers are seen widely until October. Like other warblers, the Canada is best located by listening for its song, a fairly loud, jumbled, set of chirping and warbled notes. Search for them in cool woodlands of the plateau, such as in the Allegheny National Forest, Loyalsock State Forest, and Ricketts Glen State Park. By late June or July, they quit singing and are harder to find.

Clean gray above and rich yellow below; male has a black mask, fore-crown, and necklace. Note crisp, bold eye ring.

Female similar, but much less black and only faintly streaked on breast. Note crisp, bold eye ring and white undertail.

Eastern Towhee

Pipilo erythrophthalmus

L 8.5" | **WS** 10.5"

A bulky and noisy sparrow, the handsome tricolored male towhee often stays hidden in the dark recesses of thickets and scrubby woodlots. It forages on the ground, and using its large feet audibly scratches and kicks at the leaf litter. Feeding on seeds and insects, it periodically ventures into open ground at the forest edge to feed. A common migrant and breeder from April to October, the towhee is vocal, and its "Drink your tea" song and upslurred *toe-wee!* call are distinctive sounds in spring and summer. In winter it retreats from the northern half to the southwestern and southeastern corners of the state and farther south.

Female's pale brown upperparts contrast less with rufous sides, but plumage pattern is similar to male's.

Large for a sparrow, with a long tail. Male's combination of black hood and upperparts, rufous flanks, and white belly are unique. Note white in wing and outer tail.

American Tree Sparrow
Spizelloides arborea

L 5.5" | **WS** 9.5"

The American Tree Sparrow is an attractive winter songbird, but given its terrestrial nature, it seems poorly named. Early American colonists named it for its rough similarity to the European Tree Sparrow, but the American Tree is nearly always on or near the ground, frequenting overgrown weedy fields, brushy thickets, hedgerows, and other grassy edge habitats. Breeding in Canada and Alaska, it is found here only as a winter visitor from November into April, and good spots include Pymatuning State Park, Rose Valley Lake, and Heinz NWR. Very often it is found when flushed from the ground, or is spotted feeding on open bare ground near overgrown bushy or brushy areas. Scratching at the dirt in search of seeds, tree sparrows are usually in small flocks, and when startled, give a mellow *tleedle* or *teel* call, unlike other sparrows.

Fairly large, gray below and around the neck, with chestnut brown crown and eye stripe. Two-tone bill, mostly dark with horn-colored mandible. Dark spot on breast not always clearly visible.

Gray nape with streaky black and chestnut back, and white wing bars. Long tail, and pale base to the bill.

Field Sparrow

Spizella pusilla

L 5.75" | **WS** 8"

The Field Sparrow is easy on the eyes, and its sounds are easy on
the ears as well, with a bouncing trill for a song and a sweet
staccato *tsip* chip note when in flight or agitated. Aptly named,
the Field indeed prefers open grassy and weedy areas, especially
in winter when it frequents meadows, shrubby hedgerows,
grassy fields, and lawns near brushy cover. Away from breeding
areas it often mingles with other sparrows, such as Chipping or
American Tree Sparrows, feeding on seeds on or near the ground.
Breeding birds take more insects and spiders, and inhabit higher
vegetation such as scrubby thickets and overgrown meadows
with scattered trees. From April through October, the species is
found commonly across the state, but in winter it retreats from
the north into southern parts of Pennsylvania.

Small, slender with fine pink bill.
Reddish brown above. Pale gray face
with white eye ring. In summer, worn
plumage appears grayer, but fresh
plumage in autumn and winter is
buffier overall.

Chipping Sparrow

Spizella passerina

L 5.25" | **WS** 8.25"

A delicate sparrow abundant across Pennsylvania in spring and summer, the Chipping Sparrow is at home in suburban parks, and yards with lawns and scattered tall trees. Feeding on the ground for seeds and insects, it sings from the canopy of coniferous trees, ringing out with an even, dry chipping trill. Spring migrants arriving in April are among the first signs of spring, and they are often in flocks, sometimes several dozen strong, at times frequenting areas where Dark-eyed Juncos are also present. Alert little birds, groups of Chippings flush quickly when startled, moving from the ground up into small trees to get a view of their surroundings. They are fast and strong fliers. In winter the Chipping Sparrow retreats south, but in mild winters a few may persist in the southeast quadrant of the state, especially at tree farms, orchards, or suburban habitats, and fall and winter birds are browner overall than breeding birds.

Small and slender with a short conical bill. In breeding season, chestnut cap, white eyebrow, and dark eye line. Pearly gray below.

In fall and winter, browner on face, with dark eye line. Bill dusky pinkish.

Juveniles are streaky brown overall, like other juvenile sparrows.

Vesper Sparrow
Pooecetes gramineus

L 5.75" | **WS** 9.5"

A hefty, nondescript sparrow of farm country, barren land, short grass, weedy hedgerows, and overgrown fields the Vesper Sparrow is easily overlooked. Most similar to the widespread Savannah Sparrow, the Vesper feeds on seeds amid bare ground. When flushed from foraging it flies to the top of a nearby tree to survey the scene. Sometimes it drops back down to the ground, but often at the sight of humans it flies farther away to a taller tree. It is a strong flier, which is not surprising given its somewhat nomadic tendencies. A scarce bird across most of the state, it breeds locally in the Piedmont, mountain valleys, on the plateau, and on reclaimed strip mine grassland. It is more easily found in spring and summer, when it sings from exposed perches, giving a series of clear whistled introductory notes, followed by a mix of chattering and ringing notes. It also occurs as a sparse migrant and winter visitor, at times associating with other sparrows.

Chunky, with heavy bill, streaky breast, and white eye ring. Dark moustachial stripe borders pale edge of lower cheeks. Shows white outer tail feathers in flight. Small chestnut shoulder patch is often concealed.

Savannah Sparrow

Passerculus sandwichensis

L 5" | **WS** 8.25"

The Savannah Sparrow is often best identified by its shape, size, and habits. It is widely encountered in open country, feeding on barren ground, farm fields, or lawn-like areas, near grassy fields, shrubby meadows, or edge habitat. It is a strong-flying songbird, more conspicuous than most sparrows and when flushed, it rises to a small shrub or tree, or flies 100 feet or more before landing. Breeding fairly commonly across most of the state, especially in the western half, Savannahs become scarce in winter and then are confined largely to the southeast. In fall and winter small flocks often gather, and Savannah Sparrows may mingle with other sparrows, Horned Larks, and other field birds.

Crisply streaked brown, with short, notched tail; may show yellowish spot above lores. Note fine bill with a pale mandible. Some appear slightly crested. Compare with Song and Vesper Sparrows.

Grasshopper Sparrow

Ammodramus savannarum

L 4.5" | **WS** 8"

The Grasshopper Sparrow skulks amid hay fields, weedy meadows, and prairies from May through August. Generally secretive but on breeding territories males sing on exposed perches such as wires, fence posts, or shrubs. The most effective way to find one is by listening for its insect-like song, which begins with several staccato *tik* or *tuk* notes followed by a long, extremely high-pitched buzz. Search for it at State Game Land 330 (the Piney Tract) in Clarion County, State Game Land 100 in Centre County, or the Amish country in Lancaster County.

Beautiful brown and straw-buffy. Clean buffy breast, flat crown, and stout bill. Black and chestnut spotting above, yellow spot on lores. Dark spot at rear of cheeks.

Henslow's Sparrow

Ammodramus henslowii

L 4.5" | **WS** 8"

A squat, secretive and sought-after sparrow of grassy fields and
meadows, the Henslow's is distinctive if you can manage a good
view of it, but often it stays hidden in the grass, even singing from
within the vegetation. Its song is heard both during the day and at
night, and is an unimpressive, subtle, but distinctive *se lix*.
Wintering in the Deep South, the Henslow's breeds at scattered
sites in the western half of the state from May to July. Search for
it in grassland areas at State Game Land 100 in Clearfield County
and in Jefferson and Clarion counties. Similar in proportions to
the Grasshopper Sparrow, the two may share the same fields, but
Henslow's often makes use of weedier, shrubbier habitats. After
they go quiet in July, they become very hard to find, but autumn
migrants continue here into October.

Large head, black streaked back,
chestnut wing markings, and chestnut
rump. Olive neck and face with two
dark stripes on lower cheek and a dark
wedge-like stripe behind the eye. Pale
belly and throat, with short streaks
across the breast.

Fox Sparrow

Passerella iliaca

L 7" | **WS** 10.25"

A large, chunky sparrow, the Fox is common to uncommon as a winter visitor and migrant. During migration it ranges fairly widely in Pennsylvania, when moving north in March and April and heading south in November and December. Its numbers vary each year, but during most winters those that remain usually are in the southern half of the state. At home in the understory of woodlands and thickets, Fox Sparrows work the ground for seeds and insects, occasionally popping up to perch in bushes or trees, and calling regularly. The common call is a single-noted lip-smacking *tik*, but occasionally on sunny winter days they will sing. The song, usually given from within vegetation, meanders up and down in pitch in a series of high chips mixed with lower clear notes.

Hefty, foxy red-brown with gray crown and nape, and thick gray bill.

Song Sparrow
Melospiza melodia

L 5.75" | **WS** 8.25"

The Song Sparrow is our most frequently observed sparrow, common year-round in shrubby and bushy areas, thickets, weedy fence lines, and backyards across the state. It is a great species to learn and use as a basis for comparison with other, less familiar sparrows. Feeding on the ground at the edge of weedy areas or on lawns, the Song Sparrow uses low perches in bushes, shrubs, or small trees to sing. The song is a loud *tsink tsink ooo weeeeeeee, tsrp tsrp*, and the call note is a distinctive *chimp*.

Mid-size, slightly plump, with a conical gray bill and brown panel in the wing. Coarse blackish brown streaks on chest and flanks are densest at the center of the breast. Thick brown stripe at sides of throat, and gray eyebrow and nape.

Lincoln's Sparrow

Melospiza lincolnii

L 5.5" | **WS** 7.75"

Like a scaled-down version of a Song Sparrow, the Lincoln's occurs here as a migrant and rare winter visitor, but due to its skulking habits it is easily overlooked. Preferring weedy meadows, thickets, and the edges of forest understory, they feed on the ground and are often near low, wet areas. Moving through when northbound in May and headed south in September and October, the Lincoln's is uncommon, and it doesn't vocalize often. If a Song Sparrow's streaks were drawn with a crayon, the Lincoln's would appear drawn with a thin pencil.

Crisply streaked, with a fine bill. Smaller than Song Sparrow, with slight crest, less reddish brown overall, shorter tail, finer streaks, and a buffy breast and eye ring.

Swamp Sparrow

Melospiza georgiana

L 5.75" | **WS** 7.5"

Squat and portly, the Swamp Sparrow is common in swampy
woodlands, near beaver ponds, in moist meadows, and in
marshy areas across much of the state. Feeding on seeds and
aquatic insects, it stays low but pops up to exposed perches to
sing or when agitated. Listen for its sounds to locate it, and
keep an eye out for it feeding at the edge of wet weedy or grassy
areas. In spring and summer breeding birds are heard singing
both night and day, ringing out with a prolonged, evenly
pitched trill. Migrants and winter birds give a sharp chip note,
and in addition to the typical wetland habitats may take cover
in thickets or weedy and brushy hedgerows. Swamp Sparrows
withdraw from northern Pennsylvania in winter but may
remain in the southern reaches of the state during mild winters,
especially in the southeast.

Mid-size, plump sparrow, with
conical bill. Breeding adult is
gray chested, reddish brown
above, with a chestnut-brown
crown. Nonbreeding birds are
less rufous, with a duskier
breast and a brown crown.

White-throated Sparrow

Zonotrichia albicollis

L 5.75" | **WS** 9"

The stocky White-throated Sparrow is a common migrant and winter visitor to our woodland edges from late October to May. Especially abundant in the southeast in winter, this bird of the forest understory loudly scratches at leaf litter, searching for seeds, fruit, and insects and is quite vocal. In autumn and winter they congregate in flocks, and as you walk along thickets or the edges of woodlots, listen for their thin see notes and loud *pink* chips to give them away. As winter turns to spring and the sun ratchets up their hormones, males sing a wistful song, and are usually said to say, "Oooold Sam Peabody Peabody Peabody." Some nest in the Poconos representing the southern most limit of this bird's breeding range. Two forms occur here, with some showing bright white stripes along the sides of the crown, and others showing tan crown stripes.

Striking head pattern and white throat. Nearly always some yellow in lores; obvious broad, pale eyebrow.

White-crowned Sparrow

Zonotrichia leucophrys

L 6" **WS** 9.5"

Large and lanky, the alert White-crowned Sparrow prefers
weedy habitats amid open areas. Foraging on the ground for
seeds and insects, it is at home along overgrown fence lines,
bushy hedgerows, and at edges of shrubby fields. The breeding
grounds are well to our north in Canada, but it is an uncommon
or locally common migrant and winter visitor here, found from
October into May. Often it is in small flocks and with other
sparrow species, and when flushed it flies up revealing an
olive-brown rump. They perch in shrubs or small trees when
startled or for singing, and the song is a series of clear whistled
notes, followed by a burry buzz or a trill. The common call note
is a sharp *pink*, often heard as a bird moves within cover.

A large, sturdy yet slender sparrow,
adults have striking white and black
head pattern and a dusky pink bill.

Dark-eyed Junco
Junco hyemalis

L 6" | **WS** 8.5"

A conspicuous little sparrow, when a junco takes to the air it flashes its striking white outer tail feathers and emits twittering call notes. Winter flocks assemble in many places and are referred to colloquially as "snowbirds." Though the junco is a widespread breeding bird in the northern half of the state and south in the Allegheny Mountains, it is most abundant during our colder months, particularly from late October to early April. Foraging for seeds in bare ground or on lawns, juncos fly up to exposed perches when startled to survey the scene. They are common in suburban parks with scattered trees, in backyards, at the edges of woodlots, and in other open or semi-open habitats. Across its range in North America the junco is extremely variable and different populations differ in appearance. The subspecies found in the East is called the "Slate-colored" Junco, pictured below.

Male slate gray, with white belly, and white, conical bill. Female dusky gray with dusky flanks and variable brownish tones mixed into the gray upperparts.

Scarlet Tanager

Piranga olivacea

L 7" | **WS** 11.5"

Heart-stirring spring migrants that return here in May from their tropical wintering grounds, the arresting red plumage of the male Scarlet Tanager flashes amid foliage of the forest upper story. Moving with sluggish movements in the shady canopy of deciduous, coniferous, and mixed woodlands, it can be surprisingly difficult to see well. As with so many songbirds, listening is the easiest way to find one. This tanager has a song somewhat similar to a robin, but with burrier phrases, and the usual call is a distinctive *chip-burr*. A common breeding bird across most of the state, and after the nesting season is over in July, southbound migrants are seen here into October. In autumn males become green like females, but keep their blacker wings. Look for it at the Allegheny National Forest, Ricketts Glen State Park, Crows Nest Preserve, or Wissahickon Valley Park.

Males are scorching red with black wings and tail, and a pale horn-colored bill.

Round-headed and stocky. Females are yellowish green with dark olive-gray wings and a pale gray bill.

Northern Cardinal

Cardinalis cardinalis

L 8.75" | **WS** 12"

Few birds are as eye-catching as a male Cardinal. A common backyard bird found along woodland edges, in thickets, and other scrubby habitats, this species lives across the state year-round. Feeding on or near the ground for seed or fruit, they perch in shrubs or small trees and usually are found in pairs. Spring males are territorial, driving other males away and even attacking their own reflection in windows. Both male and female cardinals sing. Vocalizations include two-part phrases followed by a trill, such as a mellow fluid *reep pew, reep pew pew pew pew* or *teeyooo teeyooo tyoo tyoo tyoo tyoo tyoo*. The frequently heard call note is a sharp metallic chip.

Male is unmistakable bright red (sometimes orange-red) overall with black face and a red bill. Crest may appear spiky or slicked back.

Female is ochre or tan with red bill, and red in wings, crest, and tail.

Rose-breasted Grosbeak

Pheucticus ludovicianus

L 8" | **WS** 12.5"

A stocky forest bird with a robin-like song, the tricolored Rose-breasted Grosbeak uses its thick conical bill to procure seeds, bugs, and fruit. Working within the mid-story or treetop canopy of younger deciduous or mixed woodlands, it favors tree gap areas such as along roads and rivers, at forest edges, and it visits bird feeders. Wintering in the Neotropics, Rose-breasteds return to Pennsylvania in late April, and are common breeding birds across much of the state especially away from the southeast. Good spots to check include Ricketts Glen State Park, Buzzard Swamp, Middle Creek WMA, and Bowman's Hill Wildflower Preserve. Both males and females sing; the song is more musical and sweeter than a robin's, and the common call sounds like the squeak of a sneaker on a gymnasium floor. In July they cease singing, but fall migrants are seen widely into October.

Chunky with thick white bill; male has red breast, black upperparts, and white underparts.

Female streaky brown, somewhat recalling a big fat female Purple Finch, but with a thick, pale bill. Dark lateral crown stripes, white eyebrow, dark cheeks bordered in white.

Blue Grosbeak

Passerina caerulea

L 6" | **WS** 11"

The Blue Grosbeak is a bird of open suburban and agricultural areas, and has been expanding its range northward in recent years. Arriving in mid-May, the dazzling males take exposed perches on stick branches, high bushes, small trees, or wires to sing their warbling song. Otherwise they can be rather secretive, but listen for the call note, a loud, emphatic *pink!* Preferring shrubby areas, hedgerows, weedy fence lines, overgrown meadows, and thickets, they forage for seeds and fruit. This species is often found in areas where the similar, smaller, bluer, and more common Indigo Bunting also occurs. Blue Grosbeak is an uncommon breeder in the southeast and south-central part of the state, and is rare elsewhere. Look for it in Lancaster County Central Park, Goat Hill Serpentine Barrens, and along the lower Susquehanna River.

Male is purplish blue with brown wing bars and pale blue-gray mandible. Heavy bill, large head.

Thick bill is mostly pale. Female is brown with buff wing bars, and often shows hint of bluish in tail. First-winter birds are similar but richer brown, with more rufous.

Indigo Bunting

Passerina cyanea

L 5.5" | **WS** 8"

The Indigo Bunting is a common sight in spring and summer along rural roads and open areas with wires, shrubby bushes, and scattered trees. Common across the state from May to October, this is one of our most widespread breeding songbirds, and the males really pack a punch with their stunning blue plumage and their sweet song. Choosing prominent perches for singing, such as wires or treetops, even in the afternoon heat after other birds have gone quiet, the Indigo holds forth with a lengthy series of doubled phrases; *spitsa-spitsa, spew-spew, clear clear, cue cue* followed by a complex set of choppy, abrupt notes. Usually Indigos make two breeding attempts each summer, with the second attempt sometimes extending into September.

Small overall, with small triangular bill, small head and short tail. Breeding male brilliant blue; wings blackish fringed with blue.

Female nondescript tan-brown with very faint streaks on breast. Note shape and size (similar to male) and bill structure.

Bobolink

Dolichonyx oryzivorus

L 7" | **WS** 11.5"

With its warbling, rattling song, striking black-and-white plumage, and incredible migratory habits, the Bobolink is a unique member of the blackbird family (Icteridae). Migrating much farther than other songbirds, it winters in south-central South America, returning here to breed in May. Bobolinks are fairly common breeding birds across much of the state, nesting in grassy fields and shrubby meadows. Their distinctive song is a bubbly, chattering that recalls the burps and chirps of R2D2, the fictional robot from the Star Wars movies. Good spots to check include the Pymatuning area, the Piney Tract in Clarion County, and Middle Creek WMA. Migrants are found widely when north-bound in May and heading south in August and September. Especially in autumn, Bobolinks are often in flocks, and sometimes dozens of birds are seen as they fly overhead and are most easily discovered by their quizzical *link* call notes.

A "blackbird" with a short tail and short conical bill. Breeding male is black with white back and shoulders, and cream-buffy patch on the back of the head.

Female and autumn male are sparrow-like in plumage, but larger than sparrows with a pinkish bill. Buffy and streaked brown, they show a clean buffy nape and throat, streaked back and flanks.

Eastern Meadowlark

Sturnella magna

L 9.5" | **WS** 14"

The meadowlark is conspicuous in spring, perching on fence posts and wires, showing off its black and yellow chest, and singing away. Their pensive "spring of the year" song is heard in open areas, and meadowlarks are a common sight in farm fields, meadows, and pastures. Using their long bill, they pick insects from the grass and weeds. When they take to the air, they appear similar in shape to a starling, but show obvious white in the outer tail and at times employ a stutter-flutter type of flight. Widespread from March to October, they withdraw south in winter, often remaining in small numbers in the state's southern reaches. Look for them at the Imperial grassland in Allegheny County, Volant Strip grassland in Lawrence County, and Beltzville State Park.

Chunky, squat with yellow breast marked with a black "V." Straw-colored upperparts; white outer tail most noticeable in flight. Autumn birds are less yellow below, more buffy.

Red-winged Blackbird

Agelaius phoeniceus

L 8" | **WS** 14"

Conspicuous in marshes and meadows, swamps, farm fields, and forest edges, the aptly named Red-winged Blackbird is widespread and abundant. Territorial males in spring and summer are loud and proud, fluttering about to show their bright red epaulets, and singing their *cong-a-reee* song. The song serves the dual function of simultaneously alerting rival males the area is occupied and attracting unmated females. Red-winged Blackbirds are polygynous, meaning that a single male has multiple female mates. In late fall and winter, Red-wingeds gather in flocks, feeding in open fields at times with other blackbirds and starlings, and large roosts form in woodlands that may number in the tens of thousands.

Male has yellow border to red wing patch, and pointy bill.

Female is streaky brown, with dark crown and pale eyebrow. Bill is sharp at tip; tail is on the short side.

Brown-headed Cowbird

Molothrus ater

L 8" | **WS** 14"

Famous as a brood parasite, the sneaky female cowbird looks for a warbler or sparrow that is building a nest or singing near a nest. The moment that bird leaves the area, she darts in and lays an egg in the nest, making room for hers by pushing out eggs of the host. This insidious behavior has rendered the cowbird unpopular in certain circles, but in fact cowbirds are fascinating members of the blackbird family. Successful in a range of habitats, they usually feed in open areas, but seek nests in forests or woodlots. Once confined to the Great Plains where the buffalo roamed, they spread east as humans changed the landscape. Cowbirds are now known to use the nests of more than 200 bird species, and females produce startling numbers of eggs each spring. It is not uncommon to see one or more males chasing a female. Feeding on the ground for seeds and insects, they take perches in trees, and sing their *gurgle gurgle zee* song, which has the widest frequency range of any bird sound on the continent.

Male glossy black with a chocolate-brown head and conical bill.

Female nondescript gray-brown with paler throat. Juvenile similar to female, but upperparts more scaly. Note shape, habits, relatively short tail and bill shape.

Rusty Blackbird

Euphagus carolinus

L 9"　|　**WS** 14"

A migrant bird of swampy or wet woodlands, bogs, and waterways bordered with woods or tall brush, the Rusty Blackbird is
never far from water. Occasionally they feed in farm fields with
other blackbirds, but more often they are seen in wet treed
areas, foraging on the floor amid leaf litter or perching up and
vocalizing. Singing even sometimes in winter, the Rusty
Blackbird sounds like a rusty gate swinging open, mixed with
some *chuk* notes and chattering. With sounds somewhat similar
to those of other blackbirds or starlings, and combined with
their retiring habits and similar appearance to grackles, it's no
surprise that the Rusty flies under the radar at times. Breeding
in the boreal forests of Canada, Alaska, and New England,
Rusties are seen in Pennsylvania during migration in March and
April and southbound in October and November. In mild
winters some may remain at the southern reaches of the state,
such as at Heinz National Wildlife Refuge.

Pale yellow eye and thin,
pointed bill. Breeding male
is dark overall, less glossy
than thick-billed grackles.

Nonbreeding birds in fall and early
winter show rust color in plumage.
Females often show gray rump, and
dark lores that offset a pale eye.
Note thin, sharp bill.

Common Grackle

Quiscalus quiscula

L 12.5" | **WS** 17"

The Common Grackle is at home in a variety of habitats, common in urban and suburban parks, backyards, and farm fields across the state. An adaptable bird, it uses its utilitarian bill to take a remarkable variety of foods, grazing seeds and fruit, wading into pools to find prey, and even raiding other birds' nests for eggs and nestlings. Grackles are often seen flying overhead in linear or oblong flocks, descending to feed on grains in open agricultural areas. Winter flocks gathering in the Piedmont usually include other blackbird species, and may rise to staggering proportions with hundreds of thousands of birds present. They are noisy birds too, frequently uttering simple *tek* or *chek* notes, and at times squeezing out their *squeedle-dee* song.

Male large, glossy purple and bronze; long, heavy bill, broad back, and keel-shaped tail held in a "V."

Orchard Oriole

Icterus spurius

L 7.25" | **WS** 9.5"

A common breeding species in the southern half and northwest of the state, the Orchard Oriole is an early migrant. Wintering in the Neotropics, it returns in mid- or late April and is seen in humid shrubby areas with scattered trees, regenerating woodlots, thickets, and is seldom far from water. Like other blackbirds, Orchard Orioles are vocal, singing a fast, complex song of chattering whistles, and they also give a *chat, chat, chat-a-tat* call. Once the breeding season has concluded, they disappear as suddenly as they appeared, vanishing seemingly overnight in late summer and gone by September. Look for them at the Allegheny Land Trust in southwestern Pennsylvania, along the Susquehanna River, and at Heinz NWR.

Small, dark; adult male chestnut and black. Note slender bill and pale gray base of mandible. First-summer male yellow like female but have black throat patch.

Yellow female almost recalls a warbler, but larger, differs in shape, and slender bill has pale base to mandible; note pale wing bars and gray-green back.

Baltimore Oriole

Icterus galbula

L 8.75" | **WS** 11.5"

With its vivid plumage and common presence in suburban parks and backyards, the Baltimore Oriole is a fan favorite. Gorgeously attired, this oriole likes open areas with tall deciduous trees, where it moves from one treetop to the next, feeding on insects and fruit, and sipping nectar at blooms and hummingbird feeders. Soon after they return in May from their Neotropical wintering grounds, they claim territories and begin nesting. Weaving sack-like nests from grasses and other fibrous material, the Baltimore Oriole hangs its nest high in the trees. Nest are frequently conspicuous, and this bird does not hesitate to nest near houses or barns. The song is a series of clear whistled *tew* notes, and they also give a rattled chatter. The breeding season comes to a close in July and August, and southbound migrants are seen through September.

Male is striking orange and black with white wing bars and blue-gray bill. Orange rump often obvious in flight. Tail is mostly black at center and orange at the outer edges.

First-year birds are variable in orange, but have some orange on breast, throat, and tail. Adult female is similar but more orangish, with dusky orangish head and back. All show pale gray bill.

House Finch

Haemorhous mexicanus

L 5.25" | **WS** 8.75"

Peppy and chipper with a pleasing song, the House Finch was once a popular cage bird, but today roams widely across the commonwealth. Originally confined to the western U.S. and Mexico, caged House Finches were released in New York in the middle of the last century, and they multiplied and spread across the East. At present they are a conspicuous part of the state's avifauna, present year-round and especially fond of urban and suburban areas. Often in pairs or small flocks, House Finches are common attendants at backyard bird feeders and are absent only in our extensive forested regions. They sing from treetops, giving a twittering, warbling song that ends with a drawn-out, rising, burry *vreeeeee* note. With their typical undulating finch flight and their rather long tail, they are easy to pick out flying overhead, giving soft *sree* call notes.

Adult male rosy red on chest, brow and throat; color is richest on eyebrow and side of throat. At times confused with the stockier Purple Finch, the House has a relatively small, rounded bill.

Dull brown female nondescript with blurry gray-brown streaking, delicate rounded head and bill. Head and face evenly brown.

Purple Finch
Haemorhous purpureus

L 5.5" | **WS** 9.5"

The Purple Finch is a strong-flying songbird seen singly or in small flocks, attending bird feeders or perched in treetops. Widely encountered in late fall and winter in edge habitat, brushy thickets, and suburban parks and yards, it is often confused with the look-alike House Finch, but Purples are large-headed and heftier, and a bit more shy and less common. The Purple Finch breeds in the northern half of the state and south along the Allegheny Mountains, in woodlands and open areas with scattered trees, often around conifers. To locate them, listen for their soft *tip* note. Migrants and winter birds are unpredictable and may occur anywhere, but some good spots include Conneaut Marsh, Black Moshannon State Park, and Nescopeck State Park.

Stocky and plump, with big head, thick triangular bill, and short tail. Male has raspberry forehead, throat, and rump. Back and cheeks tinged purplish.

Brownish females have dark streaks contrasting with pale areas, and pale eyebrow. Compared with female House Finch, Purple is larger with heavier bill, bolder streaking below, and a more contrasting face pattern. Often shows slight peak to the crown.

Red Crossbill
Loxia curvirostra

L 6.75" | **WS** 10.25"

Plump, medium-size finches, crossbills are irregular and irruptive winter visitors to Pennsylvania. The Red Crossbill has nested rarely in the northern part of the state, but is more often seen in fall or winter. In most winters, few are found within the state, but during irruption years, they can be fairly common locally. During these unusual events, small flocks may descend on backyard bird feeders and others are heard calling as they fly overhead. Adult males are red or red-orange, while females are green or olive-brown, and juveniles are streaky brown. Specializing in seeds from conifer trees, a good way to find them is by visiting areas where pine trees have a good cone crop and listening for their calls.

Dark wings. Often detected only by *tsip tsip tsip* flight calls. Mandibles crossed at tips for extracting seeds from cones, its primary source of food.

White-winged Crossbill

Loxia leucoptera

L 6-7" | **WS** 10"

A nomadic, mid-sized finch, with a medium build, the White-winged Crossbill is an unpredictable and uncommon to rare visitor to the commonwealth. Found here most often from November into February, when present they are usually in small flocks. While they occasionally visit backyard feeders, more often they are seen in or around conifer trees, especially spruce, larch or hemlock. They rarely feed in deciduous trees, but being highly mobile and strong fliers, crossbills are most often detected as fly-over flocks, moving along with a typical, undulating finch-like flight, calling routinely.

Male White-winged Crossbill is distinctive, rosy with white wing bars. Occasionally visit feeders. Listen for chattering, rattled calls.

Female White-winged Crossbill is streaky brown or olive with bold white wing bars.

Common Redpoll
Acanthis flammea

L 4.75-5.5" | **WS** 7.5-8.75"

The redpoll is an unpredictable winter visitor from December to March. It nests in the Arctic, but some winters bring invasions well south of their normal range and they may occur widely in Pennsylvania. In other years, very few are seen. In winters when they are sparse, they are mostly found in the northern part of the state. Appearing singly or in flocks, redpolls like birch and larch trees in open or semi-open areas, and because they eat mostly seeds, they are sometimes seen visiting bird feeders. Careful listening may yield sightings of flyover flocks or feeding birds, so listen for the redpoll's coarse *chitt-chitt-chitt, chitt-chitt-chitt,* sometimes followed by a slurred *jeeeeuw?*

Small, streaky. Pale rump, yellowish bill, red crown, black lores. Male rosy on chest.

Female browner with black chin patch.

Pine Siskin

Spinus pinus

L 5" | **WS** 9"

Siskins are active, nomadic, and strong fliers that cover many miles during the seasons. Like other "winter finches," this species' abundance fluctuates from year to year, but they are most common in the ridges and valleys and the mountains in late fall and winter. Found around conifers and birches, siskins attend bird feeders and are seen singly but more often in flocks. Occasionally they breed in Pennsylvania, but nesting is unpredictable as to where and when. Siskins are vocal, especially when flying, and the common call is a wheezy *seetle-lee*.

Small, with heavy brown streaking against paler brown ground color, and sharp, pointy bill. Variable yellowish in wings and tail. Pale wing bars.

American Goldfinch

Spinus tristis

L 4.5–5" | **WS** 7.5–8.75"

Captivating and confiding, the goldfinch breeds across the state, and is a regular attendant at backyard bird feeders and gardens throughout the year. At home in brushy and shrubby spots, open areas with scattered trees, suburban and semi-urban parks, it is a conspicuous bird, often feeding near the ground in shrubs and flying to treetops to sing. On the wing, its sweet, staccato *potayta chip!* is heard frequently. The song is a complex and variable set up chirps, chatters, and warbling sounds, at times resembling the song of a warbler or an Indigo Bunting. In addition to its plumage, the goldfinch's active habits, strong undulating flight, and vocalizations are good clues to its identity.

Breeding male brilliant yellow with black wing, black crown, white wing bars, and white undertail.

Nonbreeding adult grayish or brownish with black wings. White in outer tail.

Evening Grosbeak

Coccothraustes vespertinus

L 6.5-7" | **WS** 12-14"

A handsome bird found mostly in our mountainous areas and
on the plateau, the Evening Grosbeak (like other "winter"
finches) is social and may appear unpredictably during the
seasons. Most sightings occur in fall and winter, peaking in late
October and November, but they may occur almost anywhere
and in any month during certain years. Such times were fairly
routine decades ago, but are unusual today, though the winter
of 2012–2013 was an exception. Frequenting evergreen or
mixed forests, more often they are seen at backyard bird
feeders or as flyovers, giving loud House Sparrow-like calls as
they move along swiftly.

Heavy finch with thick, pale
bill and short tail. Adult
male has bright yellow brow
and belly, black crown, and
obvious white wing patch.

Female and juvenile similar in
size and shape to male and
have a pale bill and black-and-
white wings, but are grayish.

House Sparrow

Passer domesticus

L 6.25" | **WS** 9.5"

An abundant and familiar bird in urban areas, the House Sparrow is also common in suburbs and at farms. Strongly associated with humans, they often feed nearby on the ground and are among our most common visitors to backyard feeders. They nest in gaps, cracks, and holes in buildings, and in nest boxes. Once known as the "English Sparrow," it was introduced from Europe over 100 years ago and today it flourishes nearly throughout the state all year. Despite its name, it is not closely related to our native sparrows, but it does resemble them. Squat and stocky for its relatively small size, the House Sparrow has a large head and stout bill and is vocal. Usually in pairs or small gathering, they call frequently, giving *cheerp* and *silleep* notes.

Male has black throat and face, chestnut eyebrow, gray crown, pale gray underparts. Breast marked with variable amount of black.

Female drab brown; sometimes confused with native sparrows, but usually separable by habits. Also note pale bill, pale buffy eyebrow, brown upperparts with dark streaks on back, and clean tan chest and belly.

Male's color duller overall in fall and winter.

Author Acknowledgements

What you see in the pages of this book is in part due only to the efforts of others. Much of what I have learned about birds and birding in Pennsylvania was taught to me in and around Philadelphia, especially through my association with the Delaware Valley Ornithological Club, through field time and discussions with club members such as Ed Fingerhood, Keith Russell, Doris McGovern, Frank Windfelder, Todd Fellenbaum, Debbie Beer, Tony Croasdale, Bert Filemyr, Holly Merker, Martin Dellwo, and Ann Reeves. A debt of thanks is also due to Geoff Malosh, Doug Gross, Paul Hess, Rick Wright, Henry T. Armistead, and Ted Floyd for their support, edits and suggestions on the manuscript and for discussions about various birds in the state.

Above all, I wish to thank those who have dedicated their lives to studying birds in Pennsylvania, and providing a wealth of information for us all to draw upon, including the authors of *The Birds of Pennsylvania* (1999; Cornell Univ. Press) written by Gerald McWilliams and Daniel Brauning and the authors of the *Second Atlas of Breeding Birds of Pennsylvania* (2012; Penn State Univ. Press), Andrew M. Wilson, Daniel Brauning, and Robert S. Mulvihill. It is to these authors and experts to whom I would like to dedicate this book.

Of course, the words within this book would be nothing without the images to feed the eyes. Brian Small's outstanding images were supplemented by those of other superb photographers, and Brian and I thank them for their invaluable contributions. Finally thanks most of all to George Scott and Charles Nix for expertly shepherding an evolving author through this project.

—George L. Armistead
Philadelphia, Pennsylvania
August 2015

Scott & Nix Acknowledgments

Many thanks to George L. Armistead, and to Jeffrey A. Gordon, Louis Morrell, and everyone at the American Birding Association for their good work. Special thanks to Curt Matthews at Independent Book Publishers (IPG) along with his colleagues, Mark Voigt, Mark Noble, Jeff Palicki, Michael Riley, Mary Knowles, Gabriel Cohen, Cynthia Murphy, and many others. We give special thanks to Brian E. Small for his extraordinary photography and to all the others whose images illuminate this guide. We thank Rick Wright, Paul Hess, Victoria Scott, and Harry Kidd for their excellent work on the manuscript and galleys; Erin Greb Cartography for her map; Priyanka Agrawal for her careful layout; James Montalbano of Terminal Design for his typefaces; and Nancy Heinonen and René Nedelkoff of Four Colour Print Group for shepherding this book through print production.

Image Credits

(T) = Top, (B) = Bottom, (L) = Left, (R) = Right; single and ranges of pages with multiple images from one source are indicated by a single credit.

XIII–XIX Brian E. Small. XX Jim Zipp (T), Brian E. Small (B). XXI–XXIII Brian E. Small. XXIV–XXV Alan Murphy. XXVI George L. Armistead. XXVIII–XXXI Brian E. Small. 2–3 Brian E. Small. 4 Alan Murphy (T), A. Morris/VIREO (B). 5 Brian E. Small (T), George L. Armistead (B). 6–9 Brian E. Small. 10 George L. Armistead (T), J. Jantunen/VIREO (B). 11–12 Brian E. Small. 13 Brian E. Small (T), Mike Danzenbaker (B). 14–16 Brian E. Small. 17 Brian E. Small (T), 17 Mike Danzenbaker (B). 18–23 Brian E. Small. 24 George L. Armistead. 25 George L. Armistead (T), Brian E. Small (B). 26 George L. Armistead (T), Brian E. Small (B). 27–33 Brian E. Small. 34 Dr. M. Stubblefield/VIREO (T), Alan Murphy (B). 35–38 Brian E. Small. 39 G. Lasley/VIREO (T), Brian E. Small (B). 40–41 Brian E. Small. 42 Brian E. Small (T). 43 Brian E. Small (T), George L. Armistead (B). 44 Brian E. Small. 45 J. Cancalosi/VIREO (L), A. Morris/VIREO (R). 46–50 Brian E. Small. 51 George L. Armistead (L), Brian E. Small (R). 52–55 Brian E. Small. 56 Brianz E. Small (L), Mike Danzenbaker (R). 57–58 Brian E. Small. 59 B. K. Wheeler/VIREO. 60 Brian E. Small. 61 Alan Murphy (T), Brian E. Small (B). 62 Brian E. Small. 63 Alan Murphy (L), J. Fuhrman/VIREO (R). 64 Brian E. Small. 65 B. K. Wheeler/VIREO (T), Brian E. Small (B). 66–67 Jerry Liguori. 68–69 Jim Zipp. 70 Jim Zipp. 71 George L. Armistead (T), Jim Zipp (B). 72–83 Brian E. Small. 84 George L. Armistead (T), Brian E. Small (B). 85–98 Brian E. Small. 99 Garth McElroy. 100 G. Bartley/VIREO (T), A. Morris/VIREO (B). 101 Brian E. Small (T), Doug Wechsler/VIREO (B). 102–104 Brian E. Small. 105 Jacob S. Spendelow (T), G. Armistead/VIREO (B). 106 Brian E. Small. 107 Brian E. Small (T), R. & N. Bowers/VIREO (B). 108 Brian E. Small. 109 George L. Armistead. 110–119 Brian E. Small. 120 W. Greene/VIREO. 121 Brian E. Small. 122 Brian E. Small (T), Alan Murphy (B). 123 G. Bartley/VIREO 124 George L. Armistead. 125–127 Brian E. Small. 128 Brian E. Small (L), Alan Murphy (R). 129 Brian E. Small. 130 Brian E. Small. 131 Alan Murphy. 132 Brian E. Small (L), R. Curtis/VIREO (R). 133 Brian E. Small. 134 Brian E. Small. 135 R. Crossley/VIREO (T), Alan Murphy (B). 136 George L. Armistead. 137 Brian E. Small (T), George L. Armistead (B). 138–154 Brian E. Small. 155 Brian E. Small (L), Bob Steele (R). 156 Brian E. Small. 157 George L. Armistead. 158 George L. Armistead (T), Alan Murphy (B). 159 G. Bartley/VIREO. 160 G. Bartley/VIREO (T), R. Curtis/VIREO (B). 161 George L. Armistead. 162 Brian E. Small. 163 G. Bartley/VIREO. 164–192 Brian E. Small. 193 Alan Murphy (L), George L. Armistead (R). 194–222 Brian E. Small. 223 Brian E. Small (T), Bob Steele (B). 224–232 Brian E. Small. 233 Jim Zipp. 234–262 Brian E. Small. 263 Garth McElroy. 264 Brian E. Small. 265 G. McElroy/VIREO (T), C. Nadeau/VIREO (B). 266–267 Brian E. Small. 268 George L. Armistead. 269–271 Brian E. Small.

Official List of the Birds of Pennsylvania

The Official List of the Birds of Pennsylvania was last published in 2006 (*Pennsylvania Birds* V20:184-189). One of the responsibilities of the Pennsylvania Ornithological Records Committee (P.O.R.C.) is to review the status of all species on the state list and to publish an Official State List every five years. The committee has completed its assignment and the following list is the result of its work.

CLASSIFICATION OF RECORDS

Class I: An accepted species documented by identifiable specimen, diagnostic photograph, or diagnostic recording.

Class II: An accepted sight record documented independently by two or more observers.

Class III: An accepted sight record documented independently by one observer.

The records must meet Class I criteria to be included on the Official List. Species in Class II and Class III are accepted to the Provisional List until they can be elevated to Class I status through submission of physical evidence (specimen, photograph, audio or video recording).

STATUS DEFINITION

Regular: Recorded 8, 9, or 10 of the past ten years.

Casual: Recorded 4, 5, 6, or 7 of the past ten years.

Accidental: Recorded 3 or fewer of the past ten years.

Extirpated: A previously regularly occurring species that has not been recorded in 50 or more years.

Extinct: Species which no longer exists.

Note: These definitions reflect the number of years in which the species has been recorded, not the number of occurrences within one year. Therefore, 100 occurrences in one year in the last ten years would still be classified as Accidental.

DOCUMENTATION

Species marked with an asterix (*) and any species not already on the list are classified as rarities, and sightings of these species therefore require a specimen, photograph, recording, or one or more written descriptions for consideration of acceptance by P.O.R.C.

NOMENCALTURE

The species sequence follows the 7th edition of the AOU *Check-list* published in 1998 and changes made in subsequent supplements: 47th (*Auk* 2006, V123:926-936), 48th (*Auk* 2007 V124:1109-1115), 49th (*Auk* 2008 V125:758-768), 50th (*Auk* 2009 V126:705-714), 51st (*Auk* 2010 V127:726-744) and 52nd (*Auk* 2011 V128:600- 613).

THE PENNSYLVANIA LIST

This fifth edition of the Official List contains 426 species—418 accepted as Class I and 8 on the Provisional List. There are 11 additions to the Official State List since the publication of the fourth edition in 2006. The additions are given below.

Additions to the Pennsylvania List since 2006

- [ ] Barnacle Goose (added in 2008 by photographs from 2000)
- [ ] Trumpeter Swan (added in 2007 by photographs from 1996)
- [ ] Yellow-billed Loon (added in 2007 by photograph)
- [ ] Western Grebe (added in 2009 by photograph)
- [ ] White-faced Ibis (added in 2010 by photograph)
- [ ] Prairie Falcon (added in 2010 by photograph)
- [ ] Slaty-backed Gull (added in 2008 by photograph)
- [ ] Long-billed Murrelet (added in 2007 by photograph)
- [ ] Anna's Hummingbird (added in 2010 by photograph)
- [ ] Allen's Hummingbird (added in 2009 by photograph)
- [ ] Scott's Oriole (added in 2007 by photograph)

Class I 418 Species

- [ ] Black-bellied Whistling-Duck* (Accidental)
- [ ] Pink-footed Goose* (Casual)
- [ ] Greater White-fronted Goose (Regular)
- [ ] Snow Goose (Regular)
- [ ] Ross's Goose (Regular)
- [ ] Brant (Regular)
- [ ] Barnacle Goose* (Casual)
- [ ] Cackling Goose (Regular)
- [ ] Canada Goose (Regular)
- [ ] Mute Swan (Regular)
- [ ] Trumpeter Swan (Regular)
- [ ] Tundra Swan (Regular)
- [ ] Wood Duck (Regular)
- [ ] Gadwall (Regular)
- [ ] Eurasian Wigeon (Regular)
- [ ] American Wigeon (Regular)
- [ ] (Regular)
- [ ] American Black Duck (Regular)
- [ ] Mallard (Regular)
- [ ] Blue-winged Teal (Regular)
- [ ] Cinnamon Teal* (Accidental)
- [ ] Northern Shoveler (Regular)
- [ ] Northern Pintail (Regular)
- [ ] Green-winged Teal (Regular)
- [ ] Canvasback (Regular)
- [ ] Redhead (Regular)
- [ ] Ring-necked Duck (Regular)
- [ ] Tufted Duck* (Accidental)
- [ ] Greater Scaup (Regular)
- [ ] Lesser Scaup (Regular)
- [ ] King Eider* (Accidental)
- [ ] Harlequin Duck* (Casual)
- [ ] Surf Scoter (Regular)
- [ ] White-winged Scoter (Regular)
- [ ] Black Scoter (Regular)
- [ ] Long-tailed Duck (Regular)
- [ ] Bufflehead (Regular)
- [ ] Common Goldeneye (Regular)
- [ ] Barrow's Goldeneye* (Accidental)
- [ ] Hooded Merganser (Regular)
- [ ] Common Merganser (Regular)
- [ ] Red-breasted Merganser (Regular)
- [ ] Masked Duck* (Accidental)
- [ ] Ruddy Duck (Regular)

- [ ] Northern Bobwhite (Regular)
- [ ] Ring-necked Pheasant (Regular)
- [ ] Ruffed Grouse (Regular)
- [ ] Greater Prairie-Chicken* (Extirpated)
- [ ] Wild Turkey (Regular)
- [ ] Red-throated Loon (Regular)
- [ ] Pacific Loon* (Accidental)
- [ ] Common Loon (Regular)
- [ ] Yellow-billed Loon* (Accidental)
- [ ] Pied-billed Grebe (Regular)
- [ ] Horned Grebe (Regular)
- [ ] Red-necked Grebe (Regular)
- [ ] Eared Grebe (Regular)
- [ ] Western Grebe* (Accidental)
- [ ] Black-capped Petrel* (Accidental)
- [ ] Cory's Shearwater* (Accidental)
- [ ] Great Shearwater* (Accidental)
- [ ] Leach's Storm-Petrel* (Accidental)
- [ ] $ Band-rumped Storm-Petrel* (Accidental)
- [ ] $ White-tailed Tropicbird* (Accidental)
- [ ] Wood Stork* (Accidental)
- [ ] Magnificent Frigatebird* (Accidental)
- [ ] Northern Gannet* (Accidental)
- [ ] Double-crested Cormorant (Regular)
- [ ] Great Cormorant (Regular)
- [ ] Anhinga* (Accidental)
- [ ] American White Pelican (Regular)
- [ ] Brown Pelican* (Accidental)
- [ ] American Bittern (Regular)
- [ ] Least Bittern (Regular)
- [ ] Great Blue Heron (Regular)
- [ ] Great Egret (Regular)
- [ ] Snowy Egret (Regular)
- [ ] Little Blue Heron (Regular)
- [ ] Tricolored Heron* (Regular)
- [ ] Cattle Egret (Regular)

- [ ] Green Heron (Regular)
- [ ] Black-crowned Night-Heron (Regular)
- [ ] Yellow-crowned Night-Heron (Regular)
- [ ] White Ibis* (Casual)
- [ ] Glossy Ibis (Regular)
- [ ] White-faced Ibis* (Accidental)
- [ ] Roseate Spoonbill* (Accidental)
- [ ] Black Vulture (Regular)
- [ ] Turkey Vulture (Regular)
- [ ] Osprey (Regular)
- [ ] Swallow-tailed Kite* (Casual)
- [ ] Mississippi Kite* (Regular)
- [ ] Bald Eagle (Regular)
- [ ] Northern Harrier (Regular)
- [ ] Sharp-shinned Hawk (Regular)
- [ ] Cooper's Hawk (Regular)
- [ ] Northern Goshawk (Regular)
- [ ] Red-shouldered Hawk (Regular)
- [ ] Broad-winged Hawk (Regular)
- [ ] Swainson's Hawk* (Accidental)
- [ ] Red-tailed Hawk (Regular)
- [ ] Rough-legged Hawk (Regular)
- [ ] Golden Eagle (Regular)
- [ ] American Kestrel (Regular)
- [ ] Merlin (Regular)
- [ ] Gyrfalcon* (Accidental)
- [ ] Peregrine Falcon (Regular)
- [ ] Prairie Falcon* (Accidental)
- [ ] Yellow Rail* (Accidental)
- [ ] Black Rail* (Accidental)
- [ ] Clapper Rail* (Accidental)
- [ ] King Rail* (Casual)
- [ ] Virginia Rail (Regular)
- [ ] Sora (Regular)
- [ ] Spotted Rail* (Accidental)
- [ ] Purple Gallinule* (Accidental)
- [ ] Common Gallinule (Regular)
- [ ] American Coot (Regular)
- [ ] Sandhill Crane (Regular)
- [ ] Black-bellied Plover (Regular)

- [ ] American Golden-Plover (Regular)
- [ ] Snowy Plover* (Accidental)
- [ ] Wilson's Plover* (Accidental)
- [ ] Semipalmated Plover (Regular)
- [ ] Piping Plover* (Casual)
- [ ] Killdeer (Regular)
- [ ] American Oystercatcher* (Accidental)
- [ ] Black-necked Stilt* (Casual)
- [ ] American Avocet (Regular)
- [ ] Spotted Sandpiper (Regular)
- [ ] Solitary Sandpiper (Regular)
- [ ] Greater Yellowlegs (Regular)
- [ ] Willet (Regular)
- [ ] Lesser Yellowlegs (Regular)
- [ ] Upland Sandpiper (Regular)
- [ ] Eskimo Curlew* (Accidental)
- [ ] Whimbrel (Regular)
- [ ] Long-billed Curlew* (Accidental)
- [ ] Hudsonian Godwit (Casual)
- [ ] Marbled Godwit (Casual)
- [ ] Ruddy Turnstone (Regular)
- [ ] Red Knot (Regular)
- [ ] Sanderling (Regular)
- [ ] Semipalmated Sandpiper (Regular)
- [ ] Western Sandpiper (Regular)
- [ ] Least Sandpiper (Regular)
- [ ] White-rumped Sandpiper (Regular)
- [ ] Baird's Sandpiper (Regular)
- [ ] Pectoral Sandpiper (Regular)
- [ ] Purple Sandpiper (Casual)
- [ ] Dunlin (Regular)
- [ ] Curlew Sandpiper* (Accidental)
- [ ] Stilt Sandpiper (Regular)
- [ ] Buff-breasted Sandpiper (Regular)
- [ ] Ruff* (Accidental)
- [ ] Short-billed Dowitcher (Regular)

- [ ] Long-billed Dowitcher (Regular)
- [ ] Wilson's Snipe (Regular)
- [ ] American Woodcock (Regular)
- [ ] Wilson's Phalarope (Regular)
- [ ] Red-necked Phalarope (Regular)
- [ ] Red Phalarope* (Regular)
- [ ] Black-Legged Kittiwake (Accidental)
- [ ] Sabine's Gull* (Casual)
- [ ] Bonaparte's Gull (Regular)
- [ ] Black-headed Gull* (Regular)
- [ ] Little Gull (Regular)
- [ ] Ross's Gull* (Accidental)
- [ ] Laughing Gull (Regular)
- [ ] Franklin's Gull (Regular)
- [ ] Mew Gull* (Accidental)
- [ ] Ring-billed Gull (Regular)
- [ ] California Gull* (Accidental)
- [ ] Herring Gull (Regular)
- [ ] Thayer's Gull* (Regular)
- [ ] Iceland Gull (Regular)
- [ ] Lesser Black-backed Gull (Regular)
- [ ] Slaty-backed Gull* (Accidental)
- [ ] Glaucous Gull (Regular)
- [ ] Great Black-backed Gull (Regular)
- [ ] Sooty Tern* (Accidental)
- [ ] Least Tern (Casual)
- [ ] Gull-billed Tern* (Casual)
- [ ] Caspian Tern (Regular)
- [ ] Black Tern (Regular)
- [ ] Roseate Tern* (Accidental)
- [ ] Common Tern (Regular)
- [ ] Arctic Tern* (Casual)
- [ ] Forster's Tern (Regular)
- [ ] Royal Tern* (Casual)
- [ ] Black Skimmer* (Casual)
- [ ] Pomarine Jaeger* (Casual)
- [ ] Parasitic Jaeger* (Casual)
- [ ] Long-tailed Jaeger* (Accidental)
- [ ] Dovekie* (Accidental)
- [ ] Thick-billed Murre* (Accidental)
- [ ] Black Guillemot* (Accidental)

- [ ] Long-billed Murrelet* (Accidental)
- [ ] Ancient Murrelet* (Accidental)
- [ ] Rock Pigeon (Regular)
- [ ] Eurasian Collared-Dove (Regular)
- [ ] White-winged Dove* (Casual)
- [ ] Mourning Dove (Regular)
- [ ] Passenger Pigeon (Extinct)
- [ ] Common Ground-Dove* (Accidental)
- [ ] Carolina Parakeet (Extinct)
- [ ] Black-billed Cuckoo (Regular)
- [ ] Yellow-billed Cuckoo (Regular)
- [ ] Barn Owl (Regular)
- [ ] Eastern Screech-Owl (Regular)
- [ ] Great Horned Owl (Regular)
- [ ] Snowy Owl (Regular)
- [ ] Northern Hawk Owl* (Accidental)
- [ ] Barred Owl (Regular)
- [ ] Great Gray Owl* (Accidental)
- [ ] Long-eared Owl (Regular)
- [ ] Short-eared Owl (Regular)
- [ ] Boreal Owl* (Accidental)
- [ ] Northern Saw-whet Owl (Regular)
- [ ] Common Nighthawk (Regular)
- [ ] Chuck-will's-widow* (Casual)
- [ ] Whip-poor-will (Regular)
- [ ] Chimney Swift (Regular)
- [ ] Ruby-throated Hummingbird (Regular)
- [ ] Anna's Hummingbird* (Accidental)
- [ ] Rufous Hummingbird (Regular)
- [ ] Allen's Hummingbird* (Accidental)
- [ ] Calliope Hummingbird* (Accidental)
- [ ] Belted Kingfisher (Regular)
- [ ] Red-headed Woodpecker (Regular)
- [ ] Red-bellied Woodpecker (Regular)

- [ ] Yellow-bellied Sapsucker (Regular)
- [ ] Downy Woodpecker (Regular)
- [ ] Hairy Woodpecker (Regular)
- [ ] Black-backed Woodpecker* (Accidental)
- [ ] Northern Flicker (Regular)
- [ ] Pileated Woodpecker (Regular)
- [ ] Olive-sided Flycatcher (Regular)
- [ ] Eastern Wood-Pewee (Regular)
- [ ] Yellow-bellied Flycatcher (Regular)
- [ ] Acadian Flycatcher (Regular)
- [ ] Alder Flycatcher (Regular)
- [ ] Willow Flycatcher (Regular)
- [ ] Least Flycatcher (Regular)
- [ ] Hammond's Flycatcher* (Accidental)
- [ ] Pacific-slope Flycatcher* (Accidental)
- [ ] Eastern Phoebe (Regular)
- [ ] Say's Phoebe* (Accidental)
- [ ] Vermilion Flycatcher* (Accidental)
- [ ] Ash-throated Flycatcher* (Accidental)
- [ ] Great Crested Flycatcher (Regular)
- [ ] Western Kingbird* (Casual)
- [ ] Eastern Kingbird (Regular)
- [ ] Gray Kingbird* (Accidental)
- [ ] Scissor-tailed Flycatcher* (Casual)
- [ ] Fork-tailed Flycatcher* (Accidental)
- [ ] Loggerhead Shrike* (Regular)
- [ ] Northern Shrike (Casual)
- [ ] White-eyed Vireo (Regular)
- [ ] Yellow-throated Vireo (Regular)
- [ ] Blue-headed Vireo (Regular)
- [ ] Warbling Vireo (Regular)
- [ ] Philadelphia Vireo (Regular)
- [ ] Red-eyed Vireo (Regular)
- [ ] Blue Jay (Regular)

- [ ] American Crow (Regular)
- [ ] Fish Crow (Regular)
- [ ] Common Raven (Regular)
- [ ] Horned Lark (Regular)
- [ ] Northern Rough-winged Swallow (Regular)
- [ ] Purple Martin (Regular)
- [ ] Tree Swallow (Regular)
- [ ] Bank Swallow (Regular)
- [ ] Barn Swallow (Regular)
- [ ] Cliff Swallow (Regular)
- [ ] Cave Swallow* (Casual)
- [ ] Carolina Chickadee (Regular)
- [ ] Black-capped Chickadee (Regular)
- [ ] Boreal Chickadee* (Accidental)
- [ ] Tufted Titmouse (Regular)
- [ ] Red-breasted Nuthatch (Regular)
- [ ] White-breasted Nuthatch (Regular)
- [ ] Brown-headed Nuthatch* (Accidental)
- [ ] Brown Creeper (Regular)
- [ ] Carolina Wren (Regular)
- [ ] Bewick's Wren* (Accidental)
- [ ] House Wren (Regular)
- [ ] Winter Wren (Regular)
- [ ] Sedge Wren (Regular)
- [ ] Marsh Wren (Regular)
- [ ] Blue-gray Gnatcatcher (Regular)
- [ ] Golden-crowned Kinglet (Regular)
- [ ] Ruby-crowned Kinglet (Regular)
- [ ] Northern Wheatear* (Accidental)
- [ ] Eastern Bluebird (Regular)
- [ ] Mountain Bluebird* (Accidental)
- [ ] Townsend's Solitaire* (Casual)
- [ ] Veery (Regular)
- [ ] Gray-cheeked Thrush (Regular)
- [ ] Bicknell's Thrush* (Casual)
- [ ] Swainson's Thrush (Regular)
- [ ] Hermit Thrush (Regular)
- [ ] Wood Thrush (Regular)
- [ ] Redwing* (Accidental)
- [ ] American Robin (Regular)

- [ ] Varied Thrush* (Casual)
- [ ] Gray Catbird (Regular)
- [ ] Northern Mockingbird (Regular)
- [ ] Brown Thrasher (Regular)
- [ ] European Starling (Regular)
- [ ] American Pipit (Regular)
- [ ] Bohemian Waxwing* (Casual)
- [ ] Cedar Waxwing (Regular)
- [ ] Lapland Longspur (Regular)
- [ ] Snow Bunting (Regular)
- [ ] Ovenbird (Regular)
- [ ] Worm-eating Warbler (Regular)
- [ ] Louisiana Waterthrush (Regular)
- [ ] Northern Waterthrush (Regular)
- [ ] Blue-winged Warbler (Regular)
- [ ] Golden-winged Warbler (Regular)
- [ ] Black-and-white Warbler (Regular)
- [ ] Prothonotary Warbler (Regular)
- [ ] Swainson's Warbler* (Casual)
- [ ] Tennessee Warbler (Regular)
- [ ] Orange-crowned Warbler (Regular)
- [ ] Nashville Warbler (Regular)
- [ ] Connecticut Warbler (Regular)
- [ ] MacGillivray's Warbler* (Accidental)
- [ ] Mourning Warbler (Regular)
- [ ] Kentucky Warbler (Regular)
- [ ] Common Yellowthroat (Regular)
- [ ] Hooded Warbler (Regular)
- [ ] American Redstart (Regular)
- [ ] Kirtland's Warbler* (Accidental)
- [ ] Cape May Warbler (Regular)
- [ ] Cerulean Warbler (Regular)
- [ ] Northern Parula (Regular)
- [ ] Magnolia Warbler (Regular)

- [ ] Bay-breasted Warbler (Regular)
- [ ] Blackburnian Warbler (Regular)
- [ ] Yellow Warbler (Regular)
- [ ] Chestnut-sided Warbler (Regular)
- [ ] Blackpoll Warbler (Regular)
- [ ] Black-throated Blue Warbler (Regular)
- [ ] Palm Warbler (Regular)
- [ ] Pine Warbler (Regular)
- [ ] Yellow-rumped Warbler (Regular)
- [ ] Yellow-throated Warbler (Regular)
- [ ] Prairie Warbler (Regular)
- [ ] Black-throated Gray Warbler* (Accidental)
- [ ] Townsend's Warbler* (Accidental)
- [ ] Black-throated Green Warbler (Regular)
- [ ] Canada Warbler (Regular)
- [ ] Wilson's Warbler (Regular)
- [ ] Yellow-breasted Chat (Regular)
- [ ] Green-tailed Towhee* (Accidental)
- [ ] Spotted Towhee* (Accidental)
- [ ] Eastern Towhee (Regular)
- [ ] Bachman's Sparrow* (Extirpated)
- [ ] American Tree Sparrow (Regular)
- [ ] Chipping Sparrow (Regular)
- [ ] Clay-colored Sparrow (Regular)
- [ ] Field Sparrow (Regular)
- [ ] Vesper Sparrow (Regular)
- [ ] Lark Sparrow* (Casual)
- [ ] Lark Bunting* (Accidental)
- [ ] Savannah Sparrow (Regular)
- [ ] Grasshopper Sparrow (Regular)
- [ ] Henslow's Sparrow (Regular)
- [ ] Le Conte's Sparrow* (Casual)
- [ ] Nelson's Sparrow (Regular)
- [ ] Saltmarsh Sparrow* (Accidental)

- [ ] Seaside Sparrow^ (Accidental)
- [ ] Fox Sparrow (Regular)
- [ ] Song Sparrow (Regular)
- [ ] Lincoln's Sparrow (Regular)
- [ ] Swamp Sparrow (Regular)
- [ ] White-throated Sparrow (Regular)
- [ ] Harris's Sparrow* (Casual)
- [ ] White-crowned Sparrow (Regular)
- [ ] Golden-crowned Sparrow* (Accidental)
- [ ] Dark-eyed Junco (Regular)
- [ ] Summer Tanager* (Regular)
- [ ] Scarlet Tanager (Regular)
- [ ] Western Tanager* (Accidental)
- [ ] Northern Cardinal (Regular)
- [ ] Rose-breasted Grosbeak (Regular)

- [ ] Black-headed Grosbeak* (Accidental)
- [ ] Blue Grosbeak (Regular)
- [ ] Lazuli Bunting* (Accidental)
- [ ] Indigo Bunting (Regular)
- [ ] Painted Bunting* (Casual)
- [ ] Dickcissel (Regular)
- [ ] Bobolink (Regular)
- [ ] Red-winged Blackbird (Regular)
- [ ] Eastern Meadowlark (Regular)
- [ ] Western Meadowlark* (Casual)
- [ ] Yellow-headed Blackbird (Regular)
- [ ] Rusty Blackbird (Regular)
- [ ] Brewer's Blackbird (Regular)
- [ ] Common Grackle (Regular)
- [ ] Brown-headed Cowbird (Regular)

- [ ] Orchard Oriole (Regular)
- [ ] Bullock's Oriole* (Accidental)
- [ ] Baltimore Oriole (Regular)
- [ ] Scott's Oriole* (Accidental)
- [ ] Brambling* (Accidental)
- [ ] Pine Grosbeak* (Accidental)
- [ ] Purple Finch (Regular)
- [ ] House Finch (Regular)
- [ ] Red Crossbill (Regular)
- [ ] White-winged Crossbill (Regular)
- [ ] Common Redpoll (Regular)
- [ ] Hoary Redpoll* (Accidental)
- [ ] Pine Siskin (Regular)
- [ ] American Goldfinch (Regular)
- [ ] Evening Grosbeak (Regular)
- [ ] House Sparrow (Regular)

PROVISIONAL LIST

Although no species is accepted on the official Pennsylvania list without documentation by specimen, photograph or tape-recording, the Committee may accept sight records (i.e. for species not on the state list) which are supported by written details alone. Such species are added to this "Provisional List." If acceptable documentation in the form of specimen, photograph, or video/audio recording finally becomes available, the species is then moved to the Class I list.

- [ ] Common Eider* (Accidental)
- [ ] Northern Fulmar* (Accidental)
- [ ] Black-tailed Godwit* (Accidental)

- [ ] Surfbird* (Accidental)
- [ ] Band-tailed Pigeon* (Accidental)
- [ ] Apus sp.* (Accidental)
- [ ] Lewis's Woodpecker* (Accidental)

- [ ] Violet-green Swallow* (Accidental)

REQUESTS FOR CORRECTIONS AND RECORDS

This Official List should not be considered as the final word on Pennsylvania birdlife. It is only our knowledge to the present, and will be outdated soon after it is published. Undoubtedly, there will be errors, typographical or technical, and perhaps omissions. When these are noted or when authentic records are obtained for species that are not listed, that information should be forwarded to the Pennsylvania Ornithological Records Committee, Ian Gardner, gardnie07@gmail.com; www.pabirds.org/records/.

Species Index

A

Acanthis flammea, 266
Accipiter
    cooperii, 64
    gentilis, 66
    striatus, 65
Actitis macularius, 84
Aegolius acadicus, 117
Agelaius phoeniceus, 256
Aix sponsa, 6
Ammodramus
    henslowii, 241
    savannarum, 240
Anas
    acuta, 8
    americana, 9
    clypeata, 14
    crecca, 16
    discors, 12
    platyrhynchos, 11
    rubripes, 10
    strepera, 7
Anthus rubescens, 192
Antrostomus vociferus, 123
Aquila chrysaetos, 59
Archilochus colubris, 125
Ardea
    alba, 49
    herodias, 48
Arenaria interpres, 88
Asio
    flammeus, 121
    otus, 120
Aythya
    affinis, 18
    americana, 20
    collaris, 22
    marila, 19
    valisineria, 21

B

Baeolophus bicolor, 166
Bartramia longicauda, 86
Bittern
    American, 46
    Least, 47
Blackbird
    Red-winged, 256
    Rusty, 258
Bluebird, Eastern, 182
Bobolink, 254
Bobwhite, Northern, 33
Bombycilla
    cedrorum, 191

Bonasa umbellus, 35
Botaurus
    lentiginosus, 46
Branta canadensis, 3
Bubo
    scandiacus, 115
    virginianus, 118
Bucephala
    albeola, 27
    clangula, 28
Bufflehead, 27
Bunting
    Indigo, 253
    Snow, 193
Buteo
    jamaicensis, 70
    lagopus, 69
    lineatus, 68
    platypterus, 63
Butorides virescens, 54

C

Calidris
    alba, 89
    alpina, 91
    bairdii, 93
    fuscicollis, 92
    himantopus, 90
    melanotos, 87
    minutilla, 95
    pusilla, 94
Canvasback, 21
Cardellina
    canadensis, 231
    pusilla, 211
Cardinal, Northern, 250
Cardinalis cardinalis, 250
Catbird, Gray, 188
Cathartes aura, 57
Catharus
    fuscescens, 179
    guttatus, 177
    minimus, 180
    ustulatus, 181
Certhia americana, 167
Chaetura pelagica, 124
Charadrius
    semipalmatus, 80
    vociferus, 81
Chat, Yellow-breasted, 194
Chen caerulescens, 2
Chickadee
    Black-capped, 165
    Carolina, 164
Chlidonias niger, 107

282 **INDEX**

Quick Index

See the Species Index for a complete listing of all the birds in the *ABA Field Guide to Birds of Pennsylvania*.